BLOOMING YOUR LIFE

HOW TO EXPERIENCE CONSISTENT HAPPINESS

BECA LEWIS

PERCEPTION PUBLISHING

First Copyright©2022 by Beca Lewis and Perception Publishing. All rights reserved. No portion of this book may be reproduced in any form without written permission from the publisher or author, except as permitted by U.S. copyright law, except for the inclusion of brief quotations in a review.

Contents

Happiness Is ...	1
Preface	2
Section One: Preparation	5
1. Bloom Where	6
2. Why Happy	8
3. Leading Happiness	11
4. Happiness: A Shift Of Perception	15
5. Practical Blooming: Preparation	17
6. Renee: Preparation	19
Section Two: Seven Happiness Steps	22
Step One: Prepare To Grow	23
7. Decide To Be Happy	24
8. Perception Shifts	26
9. The Two Modes Of Perception	29
10. Let Go	32

11.	Gift Your Future Self	34
12.	The Good That We Need	37
13.	Practical Blooming: Step One	39
14.	Renee: Step One	40

Step Two: Put Yourself Where You Grow Best — 42

15.	Designing Your Excellent Life	43
16.	Create Your Habitat To Thrive	47
17.	Joy Is Waiting For You	50
18.	Perception Rules	53
19.	Practical Blooming: Step Two	56
20.	Renee: Step Two	57

Step Three: Move Yourself If Necessary — 59

21.	Moving To Thrive	60
22.	Recognizing Abuse	64
23.	You Can Rewrite The Past	69
24.	Habits and Happiness	71
25.	Think Like A Sunflower	74
26.	Practical Blooming: Step Three	77
27.	Renee: Step Three	78

Step Four: Feed Yourself The Best Food Possible — 80

28. We Are What We Eat	81
29. Consciously Choose Happiness	83
30. Happy To Want Less	85
31. Choose Consciously	88
32. Practical Blooming: Step Four	92
33. Renee: Step Four	94
Step Five: Grow In Your Own Timing	96
34. Your Timing Is Perfect	97
35. What The Past Reveals	102
36. Live Your Why	105
37. Practical Blooming: Step Five	108
38. Renee: Step Five	109
Step Six: Expect To Bloom	111
39. Yes, It Will Come Up	112
40. Designed To Be Filled	117
41. Let Go And Rise	119
42. The Qualities Of What We Desire	122
43. Quality Word Details	125
44. Practical Blooming: Step Six	129
45. Renee: Step Six	130

Step Seven: Celebrate The Unique Bloom That You Are — 133

46. Stop Resisting — 134

47. Go For The Goodness — 137

48. Be Unreasonably Happy — 140

49. Practical Blooming: Step Seven — 143

50. Go Forth And Bloom — 144

51. Renee: Step Seven — 146

52. Author Note — 149

Resources — 151

Acknowledgments — 154

Other Places To Find Beca — 155

Also By Beca — 156

About Beca — 158

HAPPINESS IS ...

The world is a looking glass and gives back to every man the reflection of his own face. — William Makepeace Thackeray

In order to be utterly happy, the only thing necessary is to refrain from comparing this moment with other moments in the past, which I often did not fully enjoy because I was comparing them with other moments of the future. — Andre Gide

Preface

To be a Flower, is profound Responsibility. — Emily Dickinson

This book began as a blog post in 2008. Then it became a 7-Day Shift email course. And then, like a tree, it grew into a talk that I gave at various functions. After that, it branched out into an online video course, then a class, and now a book.

As with the blog, course, and classes, I have an intention. I want to help you design your days and life to match who you are, discover what you need to thrive, explore the possibilities of happiness, and apply what you learn.

In our classes, we agree to fully take part in a community garden of like-minded souls so that every member feels the support and encouragement of walking with a group of people on the same path with everyone's best interests in mind.

I know that reading a book may not feel the same to you. But if you wish to, you can imagine that you are in this community and feel its support as you read through this book. Think of all the people doing the same thing as you. Each of you is making life better for the next person, even if you never meet them.

However, perhaps you can find a friend or two to study this book with together, and you will make the same agreement to support each other.

Or maybe I'll see you in class one day, or on one of my online courses, or perhaps you'll join our *Perception Circle* at perceptionu.com

However, even if you feel you are doing this by yourself, let me assure you that you aren't. I know that all the support you need will be present for you in a multitude of ways if you expect to see it.

In addition, there are communities of life-gardeners that you may not know now, but as you do this work for yourself, you will become one of them.

My desire for you is that your life blooms with happiness now and into your future.

But to bloom happiness, we must have the desire to be happy. We have to decide to cultivate the intent and passion for our life to bloom.

Even if you don't feel that way now, stick with me for a bit, and let's see if we can't unearth that desire. It's there, I promise.

And if you already feel it, let's expand that intent and desire together. Let's be willing to bloom profusely as ourselves—each of us as an individual bloom, but always connected and needing each other in this garden of life.

Darwin called it "an abominable mystery" — he wrote: *Look into a flower, and what do you see? Into the very heart of nature's double nature — that is, the contending energies of creation and dissolution, the spiraling toward complex form and the tidal pull away from it. Apollo and Dionysus were names the Greeks gave to these two faces of nature, and nowhere in nature is their contest as plain or as poignant as it is in the beauty of a flower and its rapid passing. There, the achievement of order against all odds and its blithe abandonment. There, the perfection of art and the blind flux of nature. There, somehow, both transcendence and necessity. Could that be it — right there, in a flower — the meaning of life?*

Welcome to the garden! — Beca

PS:
Please be sure to do the *Practical Blooming* section at the end of each chapter. Otherwise, this book is only partially valuable to you. It would be like looking at a catalog of seeds and plants but never planting the garden.

If, as you read this, you discover you would like to pursue more of the ideas in this book, try another book in *The Shift Series*. Each one has a different focus, but the same premise. The mother tree book is *Living In Grace*. The rest of the series are the branches.

Section One: Preparation

One

Bloom Where

Our mind is a garden, our thoughts are the seeds, you can grow flowers or you can grow weeds. — Rita Ghatourey

We've all heard the saying, "bloom where you're planted." There's truth in this. Because sometimes, maybe often, we find ourselves somewhere we would rather not be. And if the choice is between being miserable or happy, then for heaven's sake, let's be happy. Let's choose not to droop or languish and instead do our best to bloom.

However, wouldn't it be better to plant ourselves where we would bloom best?

I love the process of gardening. And over the years, I have learned that some plants don't grow well where I put them. Sometimes—don't tell anyone—I swear I hear them begging me to move them somewhere else.

So even though when I first plant them, I pay attention to what the plants' needs are, sun or shade, for example, sometimes I need to move them anyway because they aren't thriving. There are other factors at work. Perhaps, like people, they don't like the area, or the neighbor is too noisy, or they want a different view.

I moved a plant once that looked so bedraggled I was afraid to move it, thinking that the transfer might kill it. But I did it anyway because it kept asking me to. I moved it from the backyard, a nice shady spot, to the front yard, also a nice shady spot, and within hours it perked up and, by the end of the day, looked better than it had ever looked. It thrived there. And every time I check on it, I swear it says thank you.

So yes, if I can see plants in this way, I can certainly see us humans as plants. But as human plants, we have many more abilities than a plant does.

Well, perhaps plants have more abilities than we think, but that's for another day. If you are interested in the intelligence of the plant kingdom, I have listed a few books on it at the end of this book in the Resources section.

But I know you are here for you, so let's find out where you will thrive the most. It doesn't mean you will pick up and move yourself, although you might. It just means you will give yourself more choices that enable you to thrive as intended by the Master Gardener.

Two

Why Happy

Act as if what you do makes a difference. It does. — William James

This book is about taking steps to experience happiness, and who doesn't want to be happy?

I really should warn you that this is a trick question because although you are likely to answer, "everybody wants to be happy," but you may be consciously or unconsciously thinking that you don't have the right to be happy.

Even if you believe that you have the right to be happy, and it would be a good idea to be happy, do you know what happiness is for you?

Many of us have been trained not to be happy. I remember my friends and I being careful not to be laughing when we came home because we might get the evil eye for being too happy.

Perhaps we agree that we have the right to pursue happiness, but not the right to experience happiness, so we have never stopped to think, "Hum, when am I happy? What makes me happy?"

Often we believe that if we choose to be happy, it means that we will pick ourselves first, and then others will be unhappy because of our choice.

Sometimes we think something will make us happy, and yet, either it doesn't or has an outcome we didn't expect, like this brief story about the cat and the mice that I heard long ago.

A cat died and went to heaven. God met her at the gates and said, "You have been a good cat all these years. Anything you want is yours for the asking."

The cat thought for a minute and then said, "All my life I lived on a farm and slept on hard wooden floors. I would like a few real fluffy pillows to sleep on."

God said, "Say no more." Instantly, the cat had three huge fluffy pillows.

A few days later, six mice were killed in an accident, and they all went to heaven together. God met the mice at the gates with the same offer that He made to the cat.

The mice said, "Well, we have had to run all of our lives: from cats, dogs, and even people with brooms! If we could just have some little roller skates, we would not have to run again."

God answered, "It is done." All the mice had beautiful little roller skates.

About a week later, God checked on the cat. He found her sound asleep on her fluffy pillow. God gently awakened the cat and asked, "Is everything okay? How have you been doing? Are you happy?"

The cat replied, "Oh, it is wonderful! I have never been so happy in my life. The pillow is so fluffy, and those little Meals on Wheels you have been sending over are delicious!"

Obviously, the cat was thrilled, but the mice probably had to show up at the pearly gates again. And I bet the next time they didn't ask for roller skates.

We all have learned lessons the hard way, but it's not necessary or required. We often have to let go of ideas that no longer serve us and instead choose ones that do.

In this book, we will explore reasons for being happy, discover what happiness feels like for you, and most of all celebrate the fact that we each must be happy before the other people we love, and who love us, can be their happiest.

Three

Leading Happiness

The supreme accomplishment is to blur the line between work and play. — Arnold J. Toynbee

We milled around, waiting for the class to begin. All of us strangers except to say "hello." The teacher enters, turns down the lights, starts the music, and we are no longer strangers—we are one in happiness.

An hour flies by, and I think of nothing but enjoying myself with the rest of the class, with the grandmother from Russia who doesn't speak a word of English but has a massive smile on her face, and the teenager beside me bouncing with delight. We are all ages, all ranges of ability, all together, all laughing, all thoroughly enjoying each other and ourselves.

How does this kind of joy happen?

It begins with the teacher who leads us into it.

I have taken this kind of class from three different teachers. One marks the steps, one teaches it as if it was an exercise class, and the other dances her heart out, leading the class with joy and the pure happiness of moving to the music. It's easy to know which class I choose to attend.

Taking the class are people of all ages, from eighteen to eighty, which provides an inclusiveness that gives us all permission to be ourselves. No one is trying to compete with another. Instead, all the ways of doing it are accepted and celebrated because we are doing it and not talking about doing it.

The only ones who don't seem to enjoy themselves are the ones who can't bring themselves to participate fully. They are too busy judging either themselves or others,

The community keeps me going. If I were doing these classes at home, I would be bored and walk away. Instead, the community carries me forward long past when I would have stopped on my own. When someone doesn't show up for a few sessions, people notice and ask where they are, and if they don't get a suitable answer, someone follows up to make sure everything is okay.

All this happens because the teacher fully and completely expresses herself with joy and passion. She is adventurous and curious. Often during class, she will lead us into a different way to do the same move, exploring various ways to have fun.

However, there is another crucial point. The teacher is expressing herself with skill. She knows what she is doing. She picks the right music, plays it at the right sound level, and says the right things.

We are all teachers and leaders, whether or not we like it!

Perhaps we don't have the label of "teacher," but by living our lives, we are setting an example and leading the way. So, why not do it with skill and fully express ourselves with joy?

It's easy, really. It just takes a shift of perception.

If we approach a task—say grocery shopping—with the idea that it is a chore, it takes time away from something else, there's not enough money to get what we want, we feel overwhelmed with other things that we must do, it's crowded, the timing is terrible, it's hard to get to, oh my... I could go on and on, which I know we all sometimes do, then what we will experience is a waste of time.

However, we can shift our thoughts and perceptions to something like this:

"What a blessing it is that there is a place for me to find what I need.

"How grateful I am that others have worked to provide this place for me.

"It's lovely that I will be able to participate for this brief time with a community of shoppers who, like me, are being provided for in this way.

"I am grateful for the exchange of money for substance. All timing belongs to the Divine, whose timing is always perfect.

"What a gift that I can experience this abundance of supply and share that experience with others."

Yes, I could go on and on in this way too, and my experience at the grocery store will be far from unpleasant, with the bonus that I contribute to others having a joyful time at the store too.

As I thought over why that teacher is so successful, I came up with seven ideas that we can apply to our own lives and lift others and ourselves into the atmosphere of Love.

- Fill your heart with joy and express it openly.

- Be adventurous and curious.

- Gather a community (family, club, tribe) that supports and encourages each other.

- Make it possible for many kinds of people to find your community.

- Find a way for members to be wholly involved in their own style.

- Enjoy each other for what they are, not for what we wish they were.

- Commit to being more and more skillful at what you bring to the community.

We can see how these ideas can be applied to our home or business life, and in doing so, we are actively shifting the worldview and its activities from lack and greed to abundance and sharing.

Actually, we will fulfil the promise that we are the "light of the world," and each day will be the one "the Lord hath made."

All of this happens with no effort on our part other than letting go of what we want people, places, and things to be like, and relaxing into the guidance, creativity, and joy of Love.

Four

Happiness: A Shift Of Perception

I have learned over the years that when one's mind is made up, this diminishes fear. Knowing what must be done does away with fear. — Rosa Parks

Do you want to know something that will make things both easier and harder at the same time?

Here it is.

Everything we experience results from our personal private perception, not a "set in stone reality," but perception. This idea has been around long enough and studied long enough for all of us to agree that it's true. And if you need more proof, perhaps this book will help.

I'll talk more about perception as we move through the book, but to get us started, let's agree that life and how we experience it—is all perception.

And since that's true, let's review how perception works.

Perception is a filter. It only allows into our thinking, and therefore into our lives, exactly *what we perceive to be reality,* not what I perceive for you, but what you perceive to be a reality for you.

Common sense and practicality are essential to me. Thinking that we have a right to be happy, yet experiencing unhappiness, makes no sense. So because I know it is all perception—as do you—I have made it my life's study and work to shift perceptions to what is True (capital T).

The outcome of this perception shift is happiness. As Eleanor Roosevelt said: *Happiness is not a goal, it is a by-product.*

In this book I hope to help you plant the garden of your own life, which will continue to bloom long after you plant it.

Not only that, your happiness will "naturalize" itself, just like the daffodils I planted one fall. They were beautiful the first year, but they continue to spread without effort on my part, becoming more and more beautiful and abundant each year.

This can be your own personal self-started and well-grounded economic stimulus plan that can never be uprooted.

Renee, a composite of all of us, will be your guide throughout this book. I hope she answers a few questions you might have that I could answer if we were in a class together or if you are part of our *Perception Circle* Community.

But if you have questions that don't get answered, please find me and ask. I'll do my best to help.

If you are ready to bloom, it's time to begin—with questions, of course, because answering questions about yourself to yourself is an excellent way of knowing yourself, so don't skip the practical questions at the end of each chapter—starting with this one!

PS

There is a workbook attached to this course. I'll ask the questions in this book, but if you don't enjoy writing in your book or you are reading this on an eReader, you might enjoy using a workbook. Of course, you could always use your own paper. Whatever works for you! You can find the workbook link in the resource chapter of this book.

Five

Practical Blooming: Preparation

Answer these questions from your heart and not your head. Be honest with yourself. Take your time! If you can't be honest with yourself, who will be honest with you? Besides, it is the only way to bloom your life perfectly and consistently.

Don't forget, if you want a workbook, you can find the link to it in the resource chapter of this book.

Otherwise, be sure to write the answers down somewhere.

Because happiness is an innate quality for any being, given that it is part of the harmony and joy that is the omnipresent Divine, we don't have to create it.

Instead, we move and remove anything that is blocking both our view and experience of happiness.

Let's do it!

1. Do I want to be happy? Yes — Not Sure — No
2. Do I feel I have a right to be happy? Yes — Not Sure — No
3. Is there anyone I think would be unhappy if I were happy? Yes — Not Sure — No
4. Who?
5. Are there specific times they would be unhappy if I were happy? Yes — Not Sure — No

6. What are those times?
7. Is there anyone I think would be happier if I were happy? Yes — Not Sure — No
8. Who?
9. This is when I am the happiest.
10. This is what makes me happy.

Six

RENEE: PREPARATION

If I hadn't believed it, I wouldn't have seen it. — Yogi Berra

Renee read those words of Yogi Berra and wondered if it was that easy or perhaps it was that hard. If she shifted her beliefs, she would see what she wanted to see? Live the life she dreamed of living?

That's it? That's how it works? Renee asked herself. *Does that mean that all I have to do is shift my beliefs—or more accurately—my perceptions?*

To Renee, this sounded like magical thinking. If you think something, it comes true.

Right, Renee said to herself. *This sounds as if I am not required to do anything except sit around and imagine or daydream.*

That didn't feel right to her. She wanted to do something with herself, not sit on her couch and practice shifting perceptions so her world would change.

Besides, if that was how it happened, the implications of that were horrible. *If we think something, we create it?* Renee asked herself. Does that mean I create all the evil in the world then? What about God? Is there one? And why would a loving God create all the war and disease and hatred that has been part of the life on earth experience?

Renee recognized this as a dark night of the soul question—a question that Renee hoped would be answered soon, because she realized that these questions had been eating away at her all her life.

She wants to be a kind, generous and loving person. She wants the Universe to be loving and generous to all life forms. And she often asked herself why it doesn't always work that way? Was it her fault?

And although she likes her life and puts those kinds of questions aside in order to get by, they haunt her sometimes when she accidentally hears the news.

Renee understands that getting by is not thriving. She and the world are not thriving.

What she wants to do is thrive. Renee wonders if she changes her perceptions and beliefs and finds her perfect environment—whatever that is—will the world change too?

If the answer is yes, then again, is it her fault that it isn't like that now?

She prays the answer is "no, it isn't."

But then, if it isn't her fault, whose fault is it? Is it anyone's fault? But most of all, Renee wants to know what she can possibly do about it. Can she, and the world, thrive? And if so. How?

Answering the *Practical Blooming Preparation Questions* woke Renee up when she realized she had never thought about most of them before.

Was she happy? Maybe. Did she believe she had a right to be happy? Maybe.

In fact, Renee marked all the yes, no, maybe questions as not sure. She wasn't. But now she wanted to know why she wasn't sure. Shouldn't she know?

Renee decided that if reading the book and answering the questions would bring her clarity, she would fully commit to doing it. And she hoped by the end she would be able to honestly answer *yes*.

In the meantime, Renee started answering the last two questions.

When am I happy?

To find the answer, she needed to pay attention to herself and her feelings during the day.

What makes me happy?

Renee thought she knew some things that made her happy, as long as they didn't have to be profound or important.

As she started making a list, she realized she was happy doing it, so that was her first thing on the list.

It made her happy to discover what made her happy.

SECTION TWO: SEVEN HAPPINESS STEPS

STEP ONE: PREPARE TO GROW

Seven

Decide To Be Happy

Normal day, let me be aware of the treasure you are. Let me learn from you, love you, bless you before you depart. Let me not pass you by in quest of some rare and perfect tomorrow. — Mary Jean Irion

Abraham Lincoln said, *Most folks are as happy as they make up their minds to be.* This is a perception-shifting statement, isn't it?

If we want to be happy, we have to decide to be happy.

But the problem is, how do we make up our minds to be happy?

The United States Constitution says we have the right to *pursue* happiness. It doesn't say we have the right to *be* happy.

And that is often the problem. The worldview has trained us to believe that we don't have the right to be happy. As if our being happy means we rob someone else of their happiness. Or what right do we have to be happy when there is so much suffering in the world?

Not being happy will not solve the world's problems and, in many ways, contributes to them. And happiness, like love, is unlimited. Not only do we have a right to be happy, but we also have an obligation to find it for ourselves, which will help others find happiness.

Imagine that. If everyone were happy, greed and all the sins that branch out from it would vanish. So let's go to a higher power than the Constitution and claim our right to be happy.

But since we often believe that we don't have a right to be happy, being happy may feel wrong.

However, as we plant ourselves in a new version of our lives, we can shift that belief of not having a right to be happy. We will know with absolute certainty that not only do we have a right to happiness, but that happiness is a quality that is innate in each one of us, and we can and will find it and live it.

There are many causes and reasons for unhappiness, but in the end, there is only one way to be happy. Decide to be.

This is the good news, isn't it?

Because when we learn how to choose and accept happiness, we will eliminate all those reasons and causes of unhappiness. This means there's no time like the present to be happy, so let's get started!

We are ready for the first step: *Prepare To Grow.*

And the question is, "How do I prepare to grow?"

Just as in any successful garden, we begin by preparing the soil of our lives. Our perceptions.

That's what we are doing when we decide to be happy. We are going to shift our beliefs and perceptions.

Which makes it imperative that we understand how perception works to ensure that our perceptions work for us, not against us.

Eight

Perception Shifts

Everything has been figured out, except how to live. — Jean-Paul Sartre

As we have agreed, everything begins with perception. Perception is the medium in which we plant ourselves.

I know you have heard, and maybe even said, the phrase, "It's all perception."

It sounds great, but what does that mean? And if we agree it *is* all perception, then the obvious next step is to ask ourselves if we act as if that is true?

Because if that statement is true, then life gets very easy, doesn't it? It would mean that to be happy and bloom in our lives, all we have to do is shift our perception. It would mean the end of trying to make things happen outside of ourselves. Instead, we would spend time shifting our perception to what we want and how we want to live.

Well, it is true. It is all perception. That's the good news.

Because it means we know exactly where to begin anything, we begin by shifting our perceptions. We will find our belief systems and perceptions within ourselves and shift them to ones that help us and others bloom in our lives.

How easy is that? Easy.

But only if we are willing to make these kinds of shifts. This, my friends, is the first key to shifting perception. Any perception.

Be Willing

Being willing is always the first step to doing anything, including consciously choosing new perceptions and beliefs and letting go of those that do not align with our true selves.

Remember, perceptions act as filters or funnels. They set the paradigm in which we live, which produces (not creates) what we experience. Because our perceptions only let in what matches what we have agreed—consciously and unconsciously—to be true.

Everything else is blocked from our view. Our senses do not create our perceptions. They report them. And that becomes a self-fulfilling prophecy. We see, smell, taste, and experience something, and then we believe it. That belief produces more of the same.

You can see how easy it is to get stuck in ruts of all kinds. From the foods we eat to the way we earn a living.

Perceptions filter out what they know we don't want or agree with and only reveal to us what we have chosen to be interested in or think we need to know. How do our perceptions know to do that? We told them to.

And please note. Perceptions and beliefs don't know when we are teasing. They don't understand jokes. They don't think things through. They just filter and give us what they think we want.

Perceptions are fantastic servants but terrible masters. We have to learn how to be the masters of our perceptions.

All of this perception filtering and seeing happens at the point of our own consciousness, not outside ourselves, but within ourselves.

And we have to be willing to shift them.

We have all experienced conversations with someone trying to explain something obvious to us but not to them. The problem and solution, once again, lies within perception.

If they are unwilling to shift their perception, nothing will change, no matter how hard we might try to change their minds.

It's easy to see the block and ruts when dealing with someone else. But within ourselves, well, that is another story. Since we can only see what we believe or currently know, we will see nothing other than what we expect to see.

If you were wearing blue lens glasses and I told you the room was green, you would not believe me unless you took off your glasses. So first, I have to convince you to take off those blue glasses.

We have to expect to see something different for things to be different. We have to train ourselves to perceive more. We have to shift. Or pivot.

Since this is a proven fact, it is imperative to learn how perceptions work and what ones we agree to consciously or unconsciously.

Remember this fact: All change begins within and is witnessed without. Thought precedes the outcome.

Our happiness first begins within. And with the decision to be happy. No reason needed.

NINE

THE TWO MODES OF PERCEPTION

Be happy with what you have and are, be generous with both, and you won't have to hunt for happiness. — William E. Gladstone

It makes it easier to understand the concept of perception when we realize that there are two modes of perception; a Point Of View (POV) perception and State of Mind (SOM) perception.

We must fully align both modes of perception with each other to experience the outcome we desire.

Let's use our garden as an analogy. What if we purchased the perfect soil and then poisoned it? The perfect soil is our ideal point of view. The poison is our often unseen and unknown state of mind.

Point of view is simple to understand, and sometimes it is simple to shift. It's like reprogramming a computer. When you know how to do it, it's easy. When you don't, it takes more time.

However, it is the most valuable skill we could learn because what we decide and perceive to be true is what we experience.

If you don't know your point of view perception, look at what you are getting. This is not a guilt thing—it's a mirror thing. Don't judge. Just observe.

Remember, there are hidden points of view, ones we don't know we have until we explore, but before we do that, let's choose a point of view on purpose and work out from there.

In this book, we are choosing to be happy.

Our point of view is that not only is it our right to be happy, but that happiness is innate. Happiness does not need to be created because it always exists. What we are doing is revealing it to ourselves.

So let's reveal this point of view to ourselves: everything we need to be happy and prosperous is present now. This is a beautiful plot of soil—point of view—in which to plant ourselves.

We know that *what we perceive to be reality magnifie*s. A truth that quantum physics, prophets, philosophers, and spiritual teachers have taught throughout the ages.

And that is why I have chosen the point of view that the Master Gardener, whom we'll call Divine Love, *has done the perfect job of providing for everybody and everything in every moment.*

That's our point of view. You don't have to believe it. Just be willing for it to be true.

Now, how about our state of mind?

Suppose I have chosen the point of view that everything I need is present now, but I am not experiencing it? Instead, I feel discouraged, upset, sad, afraid, frustrated, or angry.

These emotions are all a by-product of a state of mind and they produce a poisonous state of mind. It's a vicious cycle or perpetual loop.

No matter what our point of view perception is, it's our state of mind, or emotional perception, that is running the show called our life.

We must get our point of view and state of mind to be in harmony and sync with each other.

Which brings us to the second key to shifting perception.

Become aware.

And within awareness, we learn how to recognize our state of mind and bring it into harmony with our point of view. No poison. Only nutritious supplements.

We'll talk more about ways to shift our state of mind throughout this book.

But one way to shift our state of mind fits perfectly into our garden analogy.

Step into nature. Listen. Feel what is happening. Let nature speak to you and align your state of mind with your point of view.

Remember this: perception either makes us blind or reveals what is present.

The world does not shift. We do. You do. You will choose to be happy, expect to be happy, and bloom within your life. And that shifts the world. It starts within, and is witnessed without.

Observe and witness the outcome of this conscious shift. You can prove the power of perception to yourself, and once you do, life-blooming becomes much simpler.

And that, in turn, my friend, will shift the world that we experience. For me, that's what this is all about. I bloom. You bloom. The world blooms. Joy reigns. It's possible!

TEN

LET GO

The lust for comfort murders the passions of the soul. — Kahlil Gibran

It was a beautiful fall day, a perfect day to work in the garden. I planned to move two hosta plants growing in an area that received direct afternoon sun and move them to the morning sun area of the garden, their preferred location.

I prepared the new holes for both hostas and then went to dig them up. The first hosta released its roots easily and quickly, and within a few minutes, I had it resting happily in its new home. The second hosta, planted in the same area, would not let go.

I struggled as I tried to dig it out while talking to it, saying, "Please let go. I am moving you to a happier place. You are hurting yourself by holding on. Please, just let go!"

Every minute that went by was harder and harder on both the plant and me until finally, I could pull it free.

Although now planted by the first hosta, I know one of them will have an easier time recovering from the move.

Isn't this how we are sometimes? We won't let go.

We won't let go of how it was, how we think it will be, what we own, or what we want. We hold on with every fiber of our being while the infinite intends to move us lovingly to a "happier place."

Something has to give because that is how we expand and evolve. We can choose to give up how we want it to be, how it should be, how it was, how it could have been, or hold on and make it hard on ourselves.

The sooner we let go, the easier our life is during and after the move.

It reminds me of the phrase, "what gives?" Isn't it interesting that we use this phrase as we greet someone?

But take a moment and think about what we are asking when we say, "What gives?"

It could mean a few things. What are we given, or what are we letting go of, or what is giving way to something else?

As we let go, we get the answer to the question of what gives. We discover that what gives way are limitations. By giving up how we want it to be, we can hear the Infinite say, "I Am what gives."

There have always been times when we have needed to let go and let God, but the past years have forced the issue for many of us.

Now we need to decide if we will hold on to how it was or let go and move into a new awareness. We can throw away what the worldview says our life has to be and enjoy what is being given at this moment to us.

For many of us, when a new direction opens up, instead of letting go, we hold on. It's painful to hold on. As people, places, and things evolve and change in our lives, we must let go.

We can not hold on to our material-based version of love, abundance, supply, and peace because they are not the real thing. They are prepackaged perceptions the worldview wants us to buy with our time, money, and hearts.

They are not what gives. What gives is the pure sense of happiness that is not derived from anything but from Itself. It gives completely, fully, and practically at all times.

As we let go, we discover that letting go is not painful but is full of adventure and joy and security found nowhere else.

Eleven

Gift Your Future Self

For one human being to love another: that is perhaps the most difficult of all our tasks, the ultimate, the last test and proof, the work for which all other work is but preparation. — Rainer Maria Rilke

When my children were little and Christmas was coming, it filled me with happiness and joy to prepare for their perfect Christmas morning.

Joy and happiness lay in the preparation and anticipation. Even working additional jobs took on an element of excitement because I was preparing a gift for their future self.

We can all remember when we found joy in preparing for our, and others, future selves.

However, we live in a world of right now—a world where we expect immediate entertainment. Where we are so overwhelmed with current tasks, we don't have the mental or physical space to enjoy preparing for anyone's future self, let alone our own.

But, I propose that preparing gifts for our, and others, future self is where happiness lies.

We can prove it to ourselves with a few elementary steps.

At night, as I "close shop" in my business and our home, I walk around the house and put things away that we used during the day. I am doing it for my future self.

When I get up in the morning, everything is clean and fresh and waiting for me to start the day. If I am the first up, I press the coffee maker button for my husband's future self when he gets up.

These are small happiness moments, but happiness lives in small happiness moments.

All tasks that we do are really for our future self and the future self of those that we love. But we forget that and instead think of these tasks as chores or problems.

If we turn our attention to each task as a gift to the future, they are no longer just a thing that needs to be done; they become a happiness producer.

There is a caveat here.

Sometimes we do things for a future self without caring about our present self.

When we overwork, do wrong things to get more money or power, don't take time for thinking, or enjoying the present, we are not producing happiness for ourselves now or for the future.

We may sometimes forget this, but we know in our hearts that it is true.

It's the small things that spring from love that mean the most. I think some of the best presents I ever gave my kids were handmade coupons. They were for their favorite dessert, a health day off from school, or a private lunch or movie date with me.

Every day brings many ways to gift our future selves. Would your future self like it if it was healthy and strong? If it had a cared-for place to live within?

These are things our current self needs to take care of now.

When we don't care, when apathy takes over, when it seems as if we have no power to change the future, that's when we most need to rebel.

We need to rebel against apathy and lack of interest. We need to rebel against the resistance to doing what will gift our future selves.

Right now, what can you do for your future self?

It doesn't have to be far in the future. It could be an hour from now. Start there. Keep going. Then choose another simple project.

Move a piece of paper to where it belongs. Prepare some food for later. Plan a trip to a garden. Plant something and watch it grow. Clean the closet one section at a time.

It's the little things that make up the future. And it's those little things that make us happy now.

We find current happiness when we view our day as future-self projects.

It's a win, win, win, and win situation. Choose your own personal happiness project. Your future self is already smiling in anticipation.

Twelve

The Good That We Need

In the small matters trust the mind, in the large ones the heart.
— Sigmund Freud

When I first heard it, I had no idea what it was. I thought someone was tapping at my door, but there was no one there when I looked.

I followed the sound and discovered a beautiful bluebird tapping on the glass door leading to my office. Thinking it was a one-of-a-kind event, I shooed it away. However, he came back tapping at the windows in the living room, flying from one to another.

I closed the curtains. I spoke to him at the windows and tried to shew him away. Not because I didn't enjoy seeing him, but I thought he must have better things to do.

My friend the bluebird circled the house all that summer, tapping gently at the windows and hopping up from the deck to tap at the office door.

Of course, I heard all that tapping as a message because haven't we all behaved this way? Tapping, tapping, and tapping to get something we want?

Yes, our tapping looks different than a beak at the window. Our tapping takes many forms. Nevertheless, it is always that insistence that we know what is good for us, and if we try hard enough, we just might get it.

Then we wonder why we don't.

Perhaps the door or window doesn't open because what we want is not in the house. Maybe Divine Love keeps us safe by not opening that way.

As the bluebird made his rounds that summer, I asked myself, what is he reminding me to do, to think, to be aware of, to accept into my house, my consciousness?

It was pretty obvious. After all, he is the bluebird of happiness, the symbol of contentment and renewal.

Remember that wonderful song written in 1945 called *Zip-A-Dee-Doo-Dah*? It joyously declares the present good and the good that is coming.

This is what we can let into our house. This is what we can declare: "It's the truth, it's actual, everything is satisfactual."

That summer, as the bluebird tapped at my window, I kept him safe by not opening the window or door.

In the same way, Love keeps you and me safe from what we think we want and leads us instead to what we need to bloom as ourselves.

Thirteen

Practical Blooming: Step One

Spend time with these questions. Let yourself background the answers. This book isn't meant to be a one and done event. It's an ongoing exploration, a constant tending of the garden of your life.

It is meant to spark questions and impel conscious action.

Take the time to listen for answers so that you can choose what perceptions you want to keep and which ones you want to shift.

It's not the end result we are after, it's a quality of life.
1. Is it my intent to have my life bloom? Yes — Not Sure — No
2. The two modes of perception are:
3. Using my life as a mirror, I see that I have these perceptions.
4. When do I find myself in a frozen focus?
5. These are the times when my state of mind does not match my point of view.
6. What gifts can you give to your future self?

(Don't forget, if you want a workbook, you can find the link for it in the Resources channel. Otherwise, be sure to write them down somewhere.)

Fourteen

Renee: Step One

Reality is that which, when you stop believing in it, doesn't go away. — Philip K. Dick

Renee was not particularly happy about the questions posed in this first step.

If she answered them, it would mean that she would have to think about things she had decided not to think about anymore. She wanted to believe that it wasn't affecting her if she didn't notice what was happening. Of course, she knew she had been fooling herself, but it had been so much easier that way. Or so she had told herself.

However, when Renee started this book, she agreed to be happier, which meant she had to stop hiding from herself and do the work. Renee knew that not keeping agreements she had made to herself was a dangerous thing to do.

If she couldn't trust herself, could she trust anyone? And she knew trust is an essential part of allowing herself to be happy.

Reading about how perception works, Renee could see how perception was the cause, although not the creator, of what she experienced. So if she was serious about making changes, she had first to find out what she believed to be true.

After that, she could shift her POV perception to one that made her life easier and happier and would affect all the people she cared about.

However, using her mirror as her life made her nervous. She didn't like what she saw in it. She didn't like what she saw in the actual mirror, either. Renee supposed they were the same. It was hard to remember that the mirror didn't reflect what was real. It only told her what she believed.

Although many things weren't working well in her life, she had a mostly good life. But this book asked if she was thriving. And if she was going to be truthful, she knew she wasn't.

It was time to care for her future self. And Renee realized that her future self was not just a few years into the future but an hour from now or the next day. It was simple things. If she didn't get enough sleep, her tomorrow self wouldn't function well. Or if she overate or drank what wasn't good for her, her tomorrow self would pay for it.

Renee decided if she thought of her future self as her child, she would take better care of it. Instead of her future self paying for her actions today, it would be grateful for the gifts that she was giving it.

Thinking of it that way made Renee happy. Perhaps all of her wasn't thriving today, but she could take action towards ensuring that her future self would. It occurred to her that it meant more significant issues than taking care of herself. It would also mean taking better care of the world she lived in.

But for now, she'd start small. She would pay attention to what her life was telling her and then adjust her POV and SOM to reveal an improved outcome.

Renee decided not to focus on what wasn't working but on what was. It didn't mean she hid from what the mirror of her life told her. It meant she noticed it and then did something about it.

STEP TWO: PUT YOURSELF WHERE YOU GROW BEST

Fifteen

Designing Your Excellent Life

Beware the stories you read or tell; subtly, at night, beneath the waters of consciousness, they are altering your world. — Ben Okri

Obviously, to put ourselves where we grow best, we need to know who we are. Not who we have been acting like or trying to be, but the individual, unchanged, can't duplicate, wonderful essence of us that is our true spiritual nature.

Dolly Parton, that delightfully unique individual who obviously lives with an intent to bloom, says it clearly. *Find out who you are and be that on purpose.*

Or, as a food network star said, *Be yourself; control the opposite of who you are.*

Or, as Oscar Wilde said, *Be yourself, everyone else is already taken.*

To do this, we need to put ourselves where we grow best. It sounds simple, doesn't it? But we rarely do it.

It is not what we have been taught. We don't believe that it is our right to choose. Instead, we often act like lemmings following the worldview belief system that we can, and must, all live as if we were all the same plant.

Whether or not you are a gardener, you understand that all plants don't bloom well in the same conditions. We know that a violet likes shade, and a rose loves the sun. If we made the mistake of reversing these two plants, thinking the rose liked the shade and the violet loves the sun, then we would have killed the plant or severely limited their ability to grow, let alone bloom.

Most of us are not completely conscious about what kind of plant we are, let alone where we best bloom. Even those of us who are highly successful are often doing it through human willpower. And despite our training that human willpower is a good quality, it's not. It is not the way to thrive. Sooner or later, it will fail. It's human, after all.

If you have reached a point in your life where nothing seems to work, and all that human effort and willpower is fading or entirely gone, it's a time to rejoice, not despair.

Now, instead of working hard to make things work, you can let your life bloom by shifting to a point of view and state of mind that grows your happiness in a sustaining and supportive way. Not just for yourself, but for the world.

Is it possible to be successful and happy by planting yourself in the perfect garden, life, and conditions? Absolutely. We can all experience a life with less stress, sadness, lack, frustration, or anger. Imagine that!

But first, you need to discover what type of plant you are in order to create the right environment. One place to start is with your USB. Not the marketing USB which is the Unique Selling Benefit. I mean your Unique Spiritual Blessing.

And what is your USB? It's who you are with no work on your part. It's the gift of you. It's what you can't stop being any more than a rose or a violet can stop being a rose or a violet.

Perhaps roses and violets could put on costumes or masks if they were as "capable" as we are, but they would still be what they are underneath that mask. And all that effort to hold on to the costume or mask would slowly but surely tire them into death or, at best, stagnation.

Let's uncover who you are and what you have always done that is easy for you. This means, being human, you have probably not placed much value on it or nurtured it as well as you could.

One way to discover your USB is to notice the effect you have on others. Because we are not used to valuing the essence of what we are, in the beginning, we may find it easier to notice what we consider its "negative effect."

Perhaps it often drove people around you crazy and probably still does if you haven't learned how to be it with an artist's grace.

I have always shifted perceptions, but I didn't know there was an art to it. So even as a very young child, I would attempt to shift people's (adults too) perceptions to something better than what I thought they were experiencing. I didn't do it well. I was pushy about it, and it made people upset with me.

I am learning to be better at expressing this gift. Since I started officially teaching *The Shift System*, I have found it fulfills my need to shift perceptions, and now I try to limit my advice to those who want to shift. And I leave everyone else alone—most of the time.

The idea of knowing what you do without effort is one element of planting yourself where you grow best. But there are more things to consider.

For example, do you need people around you to thrive? Or do you need lots of private time? Or do you promote change or manage change? Or do you like to do things step by step, or do you like to fly to the conclusion?

These and many more questions need to be answered and as you answer them, move your life to match the answers. It's Designing Your Excellent Life—on purpose, as Dolly Parton said.

As you bloom as yourself, you will find that you have no need or use for willpower, ego, or false personality because you know yourself as beautiful and valuable. There will be no need to put on airs, hide, or manipulate because you know who you are.

You won't need to fight every day for a sense of worth because just being who you are will feel deeply fulfilling, secure, and safe. You will feel relaxed and inspired because you have chosen to plant yourself where you grow best.

When someone says, "just who do you think you are," you will no longer answer, "not much, or I don't know." Instead, you will know the answer and be proud of it.

One very exciting side effect is that when we live as our Unique Spiritual Blessing, what we have to offer and share is noticed and desired. As Coco Chanel said, *In order to be irreplaceable one must always be different.*

The good news is that we are already different and irreplaceable. All we have to do is drop the part that is not us and let ourselves grow as our true self.

The question we are asking today is, *where is that for me?*

Sixteen

Create Your Habitat To Thrive

You cannot begin to preserve any species of animal unless you preserve the habitat in which it dwells. Disturb or destroy that habitat and you will exterminate the species as surely as if you had shot it. So conservation means that you have to preserve forest and grassland, river and lake, even the sea itself. This is not only vital for the preservation of animal life generally, but for the future existence of man himself -- a point that seems to escape many people. — Gerald Durrell

Not everyone thinks about creating habitats. My husband has been managing woods for most of his life and, in recent years, has increased his study of how all of nature works in harmony and cooperation.

The problem is, humans destroy nature more than support it. By creating safe habitats, we become part of the solution. We are in the process of turning our yard into diverse habitats that provide support and protection. We leave snags, create wood piles for creatures, and provide bird homes and food, slowly getting rid of our lawn in favor of native bushes and trees.

This idea of habitats for others fits perfectly into the concept of blooming our lives because we want to create habits and habitats where we will thrive.

In order to thrive, different creatures need different habitats. Some need more trees, some more bushes, flowers, and water. We are the same. To thrive, we need to create habitats and habits that match our needs.

However, our perceptions—which produce our habitats—look like green lawns for most of us. Maybe lovely green ones. Pretty to look at, but not very useful for the insects, birds, and animal kingdoms. They don't thrive there, and neither do we.

As we shift our perception, we will begin to see what habitat best supports our individual nature. Some perceptions that we have ignored or been upset with because they didn't fit into our manicured life might be the perfect thing to grow.

However, most of us have to plant more ideas. Get more water. Feed ourselves better. Open more space. Add ideas that we have never thought about or decided we didn't like without giving them a chance to work for us.

Every time we are willing to shift our perception to a broader perspective, we create a better habitat for ourselves.

However, when we decide to accept that we are too old to learn something, don't have time, or worry about what people will say, we create a sterile, flat habitat where ideas can't thrive, and solutions are hard to find.

Diversity is the key—both within our perceptions and nature.

We can expand our perception and create a better habitat for ourselves by learning something outside of our current interests. By listening to opposing ideas. By asking ourselves if thoughts are invasive, and if so, are they harmful?

This is conscious choosing. This is facing and replacing. This is shifting perceptions.

Creating the habitat that you thrive within makes it easier to have a point of view that harmonizes with your state of mind.

Remember, this is all about putting yourself where you can thrive. What habitat suits you best?

Have you ever read a seed packet? It tells you how deep to plant, full or partial sun, etc.

In my classes, I use several profile systems for the same reason. I don't use them to put people into boxes, but to help them learn what conditions best suit them in order to thrive.

Yes, we are much more than a plant. We are actually Infinite Beings. But in this Earth POV perception, we each have a preferred blooming environment, and not only are we allowed to choose that preferred environment, but for the world to thrive, we must.

I have listed the profiles I often use at the end of the book in the Resource channel. Just remember. They are not predictors or limiters. They are servants, not masters.

Note:
If you want to do more with habits, *The Four Essential Questions* book might be helpful because it focuses on Choosing Spiritually Healthy Habits.

Seventeen

Joy Is Waiting For You

If you begin to live life looking for the God that is all around you, every moment becomes a prayer. — Frank Bianco

One day in early May, after being away from home for a few days, I took a walk and discovered that spring in my yard and the neighborhood had exploded while I was gone.

There was a riot of color. Flowers, trees, and bushes were blooming in every hue and color possible. Even the lawns were sporting color, with dandelions and spring beauties.

A few days before, I found a note that I had carried around for years but had not seen for a long time.

It was the lyrics to a Lou Christie song given to us by two friends when Del and I traveled the country. It became our theme song.

Lou Christie sings, *Good-bye to things that bore me, Joy is waiting for me.*

Finding the note was an example of the synchronicity of the universe because we had just returned from visiting those friends.

In 2000, my husband Del and I traveled around the United States. Both of us were leaving one life and starting a new one together. As we traveled, we played that song. We were saying goodbye to what we didn't want. We expected that joy was waiting for us.

We explored the country while exploring what we wanted and what was no longer relevant in our lives.

When we returned home from our quick trip to visit our friends in the Berkshires seventeen years later, joy was still waiting for us. Spring had arrived.

However, joy was also waiting for us on the train we took to get there.

It was waiting for us at our friend's home. It was waiting for us at the coffeehouses, restaurants, and baby animal farm that we visited together.

Joy always waits for us. It waits for us as we sleep, work, clean the house, or run errands.

The problem is never that joy is not waiting. The problem is we forget to notice it, celebrate it, and roll around in the pleasure and the feeling of it.

Often it is because we are clinging to what we don't want, don't need, have outgrown, or was never ours.

Things that "bore" us.

Sometimes it's not what is going on in our individual lives that keeps us from noticing the joy that is waiting for us. It's outside events.

People doing mean and unkind and dangerous things to each other can crowd out joy. Illness, whether as poverty or health issues, can cause us to forget joy.

It is even more critical to claim joy as ours in these times. To see it, express it, and share it.

It is an outward sign of our faith that good is the power that can overcome any adversity. It demonstrates that no one has control over how we react or think. When we choose joy, we overcome, we win.

Joy is impartial. It exists. It waits for us to find it.

During those glorious spring days, I exchanged greetings with neighbors as I walked. "What a beautiful day!"

We exchanged joy. It did not embarrass us. We didn't hide our smiles, our light steps, our happiness.

In all things, events, and places, let's find the joy that waits for us and share it. It heals hearts and minds and wins over anything that tries to steal our happiness.

Imagine a world where we sorted our life by how delighted we are and how much joy we can feel at any given moment.

Play the song! Once those lyrics get into your head, they are stuck there. And that is a splendid thing!

The universe laughed at me as I wrote this. I stopped writing this book to jot down something I needed to buy at the store on the shopping pad that I always use.

What I never noticed before was that there was a word at the top of the pad.

Guess what it said. The word was *Joy*.

Yes, joy was waiting for me all along, as it is for you.

All we have to do is notice it and accept its presence. It's not selfish or sinful to feel and be joy. It's precisely the opposite.

Joy is impartial. It exists. It waits for us to find it. It's the pot of gold at the end of the rainbow. Not illusive. Ever-present. Ours to feel and share.

We all grow best in joy!

Eighteen

Perception Rules

We are what we pretend to be, so we must be careful about what we pretend to be. — Kurt Vonnegut, *Mother Night*

Since perception is the reason and foundation of what we experience, let's go through some very simple examples of how perception works before we move on.

Remember—there are two modes: Point of View (POV) and State of Mind (SOM). Let's start with point of view.

Have you ever wanted a new car and had a specific brand in mind? Then, wherever you went, you saw that car? Do you think they made more cars like that and then set them out there for you to see?

No, you can easily see that once your POV perception shifted and expanded to allow that information into your awareness, you noticed what was already present.

Remember, perception is a filter, not a creator.

What about SOM? How does it work?

Let's stick with the car theme. Have you ever tried to find your car keys when you were in a rush? You know you put them right on the counter, but they aren't there, and you get more and more panicked and upset as you can't find them. Later, when you have calmed down, you find them exactly where you left them, right there on the counter.

You were blind to their presence in that rushed and worried state of mind. This is called Perception Blindness.

Now, in the middle of that rush and worry if you would say to yourself and completely embrace the point of view that nothing is ever lost because what we are today calling the Master Gardener, which fills all space, cannot lose anything—and relax into that awareness, that state of mind—and listen to the voice within that guides, at that moment the key's presence may become crystal clear.

I could tell you countless stories of doing just that and then, without conscious thought, walking straight to the item I thought I had lost. Once, after missing my keys for days and searching the entire house, I stopped looking for my keys. Instead, I sat still, letting in the idea of the omnipresence of Infinite Intelligence. I paused, observed, and listened.

Within minutes, I walked to our front porch and, without thinking about it, stuck my hand down into the watering pot I kept there. It did not surprise me to find my keys inside where my youngest daughter, who was two at the time, had put them.

Here's an example of a POV perception and a SOM perception not matching, and one I know all of us experience at least once in a while.

Let's say that our point of view we have chosen is that we have all that we need at every moment. Ah, sounds good. Then we sit down to pay bills. Even before we begin, our state of mind perception often shifts. And if we perceive ourselves to be in a lean time, then as we pay our bills, our state of mind may go from mild discomfort to deep fear.

Once again, remember, perception is a filter, not a creator. No matter what your point of view or state of mind is, it does not create or change anything within the big R Reality of the Master Gardener.

This is a relief because that means the only "job" we have is to shift our perception.

Which brings me to the idea of frozen focus.

Since *what we perceive to be reality magnifies* if we freeze our focus on what is not working, what do we get? More of what is not working.

Don't choose a perception that is frozen on the tiny pinpoint of what is not working. Instead, expand your perception into an awareness of the allness of the Infinite, where everything is already perfect.

When I first wrote the Blooming Your Life course, I was alternating between hours working at my desk to hours working in our yard. It was very early spring, and there was much to be done to prepare the plants for blooming. I had to rake up the leaves I had piled on for winter protection and pick up lots of limbs of trees that had fallen during the winter.

Uncovering hidden perceptions is much the same. We design our lives through conscious and unconscious points of view and states of mind. Uncovering them and keeping only those we wish to experience is part of preparing to grow.

So now we are standing on common ground. The soil is ready for us! We understand perception a bit more, and we have chosen our intent—to grow and bloom profusely.

We are prepared to grow!

Nineteen

Practical Blooming: Step Two

The greatest happiness of life is the conviction that we are loved—loved for ourselves, or rather, loved in spite of ourselves.
— Victor Hugo

Learning to love ourselves is the focus of these questions. Let it be true that the unique spiritual blessing that you are is a wonderful thing. It's what you are here to do. We need you to do it. Bloom as yourself! It's the place where you grow best!

Remember, these questions are not one and done. Blooming as your USB is a life's work. But like every well-tended garden, it gets more beautiful every year.

1. What is it I can't stop myself from doing?
2. What did I do when I was young that I loved to do?
3. What is it I do that is easy for me?
4. What is my effect on other people?
5. Reviewing my life, I see this was the common element in everything that I did.
6. This is my Unique Spiritual Blessing
7. What is my frozen focus?
8. Is this frozen focus true?
Yes — Not Sure — No

Twenty

Renee: Step Two

Today I decided to forgive you. Not because you apologized or because you acknowledged the pain that you caused me, but because my soul desires peace. — Najua Zebain

Renee didn't like the question, "What can't you stop yourself from doing?" Renee figured whatever it was, it was probably something she shouldn't be doing. She already felt guilty most of the time. She wanted no more of that.

Besides feeling guilty, Renee also felt as if she was always mad at herself for what she couldn't stop doing. She couldn't stop herself from overeating, sleeping too much, and watching too much TV.

So after reading the question, Renee spent a few days berating herself for her inability to stop herself from doing what she didn't want to do in the first place.

On the third day of looking at the questions, it occurred to Renee that perhaps she was approaching the question from the wrong perception. She believed she enjoyed eating, sleeping, and watching TV too much because it gave her pleasure.

But then, maybe, in the long run, these overindulgences didn't give her pleasure, didn't bring her joy. They only made her mad at herself.

And that realization made Renee look at the question again. *That can't be what the question means,* Renee thought.

So Renee reworded the question for herself. She asked herself what she couldn't stop herself from doing that always made her happy, even if she didn't think it was valuable or others didn't like that she did it.

The first thing she thought of was how much pleasure she got from making things better. Which often drove other people crazy. But she had to admit that she loved doing it and often did it despite what other people felt about it.

Perhaps I only need to learn to do it more gracefully and always make sure that I am not interfering with other people's lives, Renee thought.

Once Renee answered truthfully that she would love it, she knew she was on the right track.

After that, she started paying more attention to what she always enjoyed doing. Sometimes it was simple things like doodling (*don't doodle on your tests,* Renee heard a teacher from long ago say), and she smiled. Yes, she loved doodling.

Renee had a long list of things she loved doing by the end of the week. Things she had told herself to stop doing because either other people didn't like them, or she thought that because they were so easy for her to do, they weren't important.

The idea that she might have gotten it backward, that Life gave her those gifts and wanted her to do them, brought her joy. She decided to look at how to do more of the joyful things, which gave her a lot less time to do the things that brought her temporary relief from what she was realizing had been a boring life.

It was a life she had accepted as her own. But not anymore. She would start growing where she grew best, doing what she loved to do. And she couldn't wait to find out what that would be.

STEP THREE: MOVE YOURSELF IF NECESSARY

Twenty-One

Moving To Thrive

If seeds in the black earth can turn into such beautiful flowers, what might not the heart of man become in its long journey toward the stars? — C. K. Chesterton

Have you ever said to someone, "Why do you stay in that job, relationship, or situation? Why don't you leave?"

Perhaps someone has said it to you. The answer is always the same, no matter what words they use. "I would if I could, but I can't."

Here's the problem. Usually, "bad" or abusive situations are not evident at first. Or we didn't know ourselves well when we first chose the location. So we settle in, put down some roots, and then discover we have been planted where we will not thrive.

Bad situations are always abusive. Abusive situations sap our life and desires from us. They change our point of view and, of course, our state of mind.

Actually, that is the intention of an abusive situation. If we have no life or hope left, we will stay to get more abuse.

Abuse takes many forms.

It is not only physical abuse, but also verbal abuse, yelling, demanding, and degradation.

This abuse is not always from the outside in. It is often from the inside out.

We are all abusive to ourselves in the name of trying to "be good." It is impossible to be as good as the abusive voice in our head—which is not us—claims we must be.

To escape from this situation and find freedom, we must return to the perception we began this garden walk with—because we all know now that *what we perceive to be reality magnifies.* Perception has a guarantee of delivery. It will work in our favor rather than against us when we choose and act from the Reality we wish to experience.

Here's our point of view:

There is only omnipresent Good. Therefore, we are good now and experiencing good now. What appears as not good is the illusion that good is not present.

We have never left omnipresent Good. We have never been less than perfect. We have never been stupid, evil, or bad.

In what we call the big R Reality—which is the Truth of our being—the "bad" story we have been telling ourselves has never been told.

Beginning with this point of view and bringing our state of mind into harmony with it, we can move ourselves if necessary.

When someone else cannot move themselves because they are lost in the worldview's illusion of not enough, or drowning in sorrow, we can rent the van, drive the car, pack the boxes, hold their hand, and stand by them until they regain the sense of themselves.

However, if we force them to move, we are the abuser. See the difference?

Begin with what is True. That will always adjust the situation, and solutions will become obvious.

We can never discover what is good by studying bad and remaining in it. When we begin with good, we can easily see what is wrong. Then we can correct it because by standing with good and in good, we have the strength to move away from what is not good for us. In good, we find the courage to ask for help when we need it.

Once we put down roots into where we do not bloom well, it may feel hard to dig ourselves up and move. Yes, it may—no, it will—be disruptive. Digging out and moving a plant requires some effort. Dirt flies all over the place. Some roots may get left behind. New holes must be dug and old ones filled.

Trust the process of the perception of all good. The disruption will pass, and the sooner we let go and stop holding on to what was and never will be, the easier the re-potting and planting will become.

All newly planted plants must be well watered and well taken care of. When you move yourself, be kind to yourself. Make sure that the basics of your care are handled. There is no need to worry about immediately producing huge blooms. They will come.

While working in the garden one spring, I noticed a plant we had planted in the fall looking very bedraggled. I asked the plant if it would prefer to move to a different place in the yard.

I am constantly moving plants. They need me to do it for them. But you don't.

You can choose to learn more about yourself and your preferences. You can recognize your own seasons of life and move yourself. Of course, this doesn't necessarily—or often—mean moving physically, but move what you do and how you do it.

If what you learn about yourself doesn't feel right, look again. Turn from what others expect of you, what life has required of you, and listen within to yourself and your true feelings and desires.

Once you have found a more comfortable environment, thriving becomes easier.

This step asks us to do something that we often resist doing, even if we know we need to do it order to thrive. But as you make that choice for yourself, it makes it easier for others to do the same. Move yourself if necessary. In the end, you will be glad you did.

Some plants bloom immediately. Others take time. Trust the process. But move yourself if necessary. And sometimes we don't have to move at all, the situation can change, and we are no longer in the wrong place.

I talk more about this idea, especially about relationships, in my book, *Living in Grace: The Shift To Spiritual Perception*.

Twenty-Two

Recognizing Abuse

It is no exaggeration to say that every human being is hypnotized to some extent, either by ideas he has uncritically accepted from others, or by ideas he has repeated to himself or convinced himself are true. —Maxwell Maltz

Because it is sometimes hard to recognize abuse, and it is so imperative to do so, I am including this chapter from *Living In Grace: Chapter 10: Obsessive Vigilance* in this book.

Recognizing abuse in all its forms, even before it becomes abusive, is something we all need to become masters of. And abuse always involves a form of hypnotism. So knowing how that works can stop it before it starts.

When I was in my first year of college, my philosophy teacher gave us the Four Steps of Hypnotism. If we analyze these, we can see how we have agreed to participate in our own hypnotism, or how we succumb to the master hypnotists, our culture, and the worldview.

1. Agree to play by their rules.

This first step is so important. We agree to take part in someone else's stated rules. This is consent. Consent in any culture constitutes contagion. We know it as the power of suggestion.

In October 1998, Oprah staged a demonstration on her show. She told her audience as they were waiting for the show to begin that they were going to release a strong odor. They were told this repeatedly. Although they never released an odor, some of the audience members gave detailed descriptions of what it smelled like.

We agree constantly to the rules that our families, friends, and the world have made. What makes them true? Nothing at all, except our agreement. We have agreed to play by "their" rules in order to fit in and survive.

2. Agree to something that you know is not true.

The stereotypical hypnotist tells patients they are sleepy. They agree even if it is not true. How many times daily do we agree to something we know is not true? For example, an overwhelming number of us have agreed that there is not enough—of anything. We believe and accept the worldview of lack. We don't have enough time, money, love, patience, joy, peace, food, pleasure, understanding…Yes? And yet, in the core of our being, we know this is not true.

Even if we have had only the briefest glimpse of God's State of Grace, we know that there is an infinite amount of everything. In every glimpse of God, we gain a deeper conviction that the Infinite Loving One is All, and as Its reflection, we have all that It is.

3. Turn your thought inward.

This is a surprising part of hypnotism, but on closer analysis, the truth of it appears. What the hypnotist is asking us to do is close our eyes and become alone. When we pull back and turn inward to where we no longer feel the connection to others, we have separated ourselves from Divine Love. In this state of mind, we isolate ourselves, thinking no one would understand.

We hide in our homes and our bodies so that we will not have to participate or come out and play. When things get worse, instead of seeking help outside ourselves, we retreat, hoping no one will notice. Actually, we believe that no one is noticing, and that's why we retreat. Like babies who think they are hidden when they cover their eyes, we think that when we can't see out, no one can see in.

This state of mind keeps us from seeking both physical and spiritual assistance. Hypnotic suggestion gains power when we are isolated.

4. Agree not to do something that you know you can do.

Finally, our hypnotist says something like, "You can't raise your arm." We agree even though we know we can raise it. Think back. What did you love to do as a child that you thought you were pretty good at? Did anyone ever tell you either that you couldn't do it or that it just wasn't done the way you wanted to do it, and you agreed?

When I started college, I thought about being an architect. A counselor actually took me around the college and showed me the rooms where the architects were studying, so that I could see that they were all men. He also reminded me that my weakness was math, and of course, I would need a lot of that. Without a fight, I backed off and switched to interior design. This turned out not to be what I wanted, and I continued to switch majors for a while, looking for what felt right. It might have been architecture if someone had encouraged me, or if I had not already agreed that I could not do it.

Let's wake up to Truth. To correct a habit or move into Truth does not involve more hypnotism. Using hypnotism to cure something is like altering a shadow. It is trying to solve what appears as a physical problem with another, even deeper physical problem. Let's add more light to whatever appears as a problem. We are waking out of our darkness and moving into light, not fixing a symptom.

Break the spell.

To break a spell, whether cast intentionally or unintentionally, we must first recognize that it is not a spell at all. It is only a suggestion, an illusion. It has no power but the power we give it by believing in its reality. Remember, since there is only One power—God—then there is no reason to fear another power that actually does not exist.

If someone says we can't do something, we don't have to agree. We start first with who we truly are—each of us is the expression of Divine Mind. We listen to the Angel Ideas' guidance as to our motivation. We declare what we know to be True, and the spell is broken.

Sometimes the hardest thing to do is to continue stating and believing that we do know even when it feels like we don't. Repeating to ourselves "I don't know" puts us into the hypnotic mental state of not knowing.

Wake up. State that you do know. Don't continue to fall into the loop of untrue suggestions. In the core of yourself, you know. There is no other Truth.

Since we are the Am in I Am, we do know. When the spell is broken, we will remember.

Do not believe what your teacher tells you merely out of respect for the teacher. —Buddha

Twenty-Three

You Can Rewrite the Past

The universe is made of stories, not of atoms. — Muriel Rukeyser

When I was a teenager, I alternated between happiness and depression. When I was depressed, I wrote poems about depression and left them around where I was sure my mom would see them since I believed that much of my unhappiness was my parents' fault.

Perhaps all teenagers think it's their parents' fault that they are unhappy. But we are adults now and able to take full responsibility for our own happiness.

To shift our past perceptions affecting our current happiness, we can "revisit" scenes from the past and see them through fresh eyes.

Instead of the person we were then, we can be the wiser awareness that we are now.

Don't worry about which scene from the past is the most important; just take the one that occurs to you now and re-see it. Rewrite it.

Visit it now as an aware adult who understands that Divine Love has always been present.

See it with the Truth that you have never been abandoned, betrayed, or damaged.

Yes, I know that because our human nature is often fixated on the negative, we may want to remember what wasn't good. However, if we want to be happy, we need to rewrite the script.

It is not changing Truth. It is re-seeing what happened as a lie about the Truth.

You'll get better at this as you let go of the idea that what happened was real and must be suffered for or paid for. It's not, and it doesn't.

What can you lose? Try out a scene and see what happens.

Move on to the next one. Would you rather be right about the past or happy in the present? You choose.

Twenty-Four

Habits and Happiness

Facts do not cease to exist because they are ignored. — Aldous Huxley

Every week for over six years, I made up a big pot of mixed spices, nuts, fruit, and grains that Del and I enjoy eating. I used a Teflon-coated pot and a spoon that wouldn't scratch the Teflon coating for the first four years. The spoon was the perfect height for the pot.

Then Del bought me a new pot. It wasn't Teflon, and it was six inches taller than the first one. However, I continued to use the same spoon, even though it meant I had to reach down into the pot to get the spoon to work.

Then one day, that spoon was dirty, so I picked up a long metal spoon, stuck it in the pot, and started stirring. It was the perfect spoon, the perfect height, for that new pot.

It took me two years to stop using something that no longer worked for the situation and switch to something that did. I was stuck in an unthinking habit.

On a visit to my mom, we decided to watch a football game together. It meant that we couldn't go to a movie that she wanted to see because she would miss the beginning of the game.

No amount of persuasion would get her to agree to let us record the game so that we could do both. Why? Because in her world, we should only watch football live—commercials and all.

I wanted to change her mind, but she was happy with her habit. I had to choose to change my idea about what I wanted her to want, which, in truth, I resisted mightily, so I wasn't happy. I forgot to choose happy.

One year, I had to make an alternative choice about what I wanted to do each morning. I have always told myself that because mornings are my favorite time, that is the only time of the day I can write.

However, I found a Pilates class I wanted to take three mornings a week, and Del needed me to help him with his Taiji class that he taught two mornings a week. And since one morning was a morning we coached, that left only one morning a week to write—if I could only write in the morning.

I had to make a choice. I could choose not to do the classes. That choice didn't make me happy. I could choose not to write, except one morning a week. That choice didn't make me happy.

I could choose to change my mind about when I can write. That choice made me happy. It also proved to be much easier than I thought. So during that time of other morning obligations, I wrote at all times, fitting it between everything else I was doing.

When Del taught that early morning Taiji class, people would tell us they couldn't come to the class because it was too early in the morning. They were in the habit of getting up later.

Because it is so much easier to see the obvious set of choices for other people than the ones we make for ourselves, I kept wanting to convince them that, of course, they could change that habit.

This is where my habit was getting in the way. My habit of thinking that what makes me happy would make others happy.

We all get to choose what we want to do that makes us happy.

However, here's the deal with the spoon and the pot and the change of time about writing—too often, we don't notice what is working and what is not working.

This is where pausing and examining if what we did before is what works for us now is valuable. This way, we can consciously choose the activity and resources that mean the most to us and not default to an old habit that no longer serves us.

Choices and habits. Let's be clear about the ones we are making. Choose the ones that make us happy and let others make the choices that make them happy.

Simple, right?

Twenty-Five

Think Like A Sunflower

Don't be seduced into thinking that that which does not make a profit is without value. — Arthur Miller

When their season was over, I pulled out the peas I had diligently planted and tended and discovered a sunflower.

I smiled at it, wondering how it got there. Perhaps a bird or a squirrel or even the wind left a single seed to grow sheltered and nourished by the peas.

It smiled back at me, its bright yellow face bobbing in the wind, and said, "It's so easy to be me."

"Well, of course, it is," I said—out loud because no one was around to hear me talking to a sunflower.

"You know what you are from the beginning. Everything you are is contained in your seed, which is amazing if you think about it. All a plant needs are the right conditions to grow. That's its impulse. To grow and thrive."

"What makes you so different?" The sunflower asked, and then left me to think my thoughts as she raised her face to the sun and danced in the wind. She was done talking.

It's a great question.

What makes us different from the rest of nature that becomes what it is with ease? A duck doesn't try to be a fox. A rose doesn't want to be an oak tree.

Perhaps it's our freedom to choose.

And within the freedom of choice, we make life hard. We accept that life is about getting things, becoming somebody, earning a living, and proving our worth.

We try to be something other than what we are. We conclude that things that are easy for us to do can't be worth much.

It's a strange worldview we have agreed to accept. If it's not hard to do, it's not worth it. If we aren't suffering, we don't deserve it.

These beliefs cause immense pain and stress because we believe doing what is easy for us to be and do doesn't count. Instead, it has become easy not to do what is easy for us to do. It has become easy to forget who we are and what we express in the world is contained in our "seed," just as it is within the sunflower.

As a child, I knew myself as a writer. Yet, as an adult, I ran away from it for years because people told me I could never make money as a writer. As if that was the reason to write in the first place. Or if nobody reads what I write, it doesn't have any value.

I also knew myself as a dancer. I would dance at night in my room after everyone went to bed, singing little songs to myself. But that didn't mean I didn't have to work at becoming a decent dancer. Years of daily classes. Years of practice to learn how to express well what was easy for me to be. But I loved it because it was who I was.

The same goes for writing. Although I knew myself as a writer, it doesn't mean I was born good at it. Every day I work at becoming a better one. I take classes, go to conferences, study programs, and listen to podcasts. And I read a lot of books. (Seriously, reading is a must for a writer and has to be the one thing that makes me say at least once a week, "I have to read," and laugh because it is one of my favorite things to do.)

Just as the sunflower needed all the right conditions to grow and thrive, our "working at" whatever is easy for us to be provides us with all the right conditions. We have the same impulse as all of life—to grow and thrive.

What is easy for you to be? What has always been easy for you? That's the valuable gift to the world that you offer. Choose that and then do the work to be good at it, for the joy and freedom of being yourself.

One more thing. Why not look at everything you do and ask yourself, "How can I make this easier?"

This question alone, asked a few times a day, opens up imagination and curiosity, and breaks the habit of accepting the false worldview that life is hard or not worth it.

Make the sunflower's words your words. Say, "It's so easy to be me."

And then perhaps lift your face to the sun, sway with the wind, and smile. It's easy to do. And that's how it's supposed to be.

Twenty-Six

Practical Blooming: Step Three

After you answer these questions, why not spend a little time, and rewrite a story that you have believed to be true. We know that memory is fluid. Nothing is as we remembered. So why not re-remember something, and write a new story for it? Make it a good one.

Note: This is not a writing assignment. Grammar, punctuation, and full sentences are unnecessary. This story is only for you. Don't let the editor-mind take over and try to write the story. Use your imagination.

1. Whose fault is it that I am unhappy?
2. Why?
3. Is that true?
4. What situation would I like to leave or change?
5. Why?
6. What are the reasons I can't leave or change it?
7. What does the voice in my head say about me?
8. This is how I would describe my perfect blooming life.

(Don't forget, if you want a workbook, you can find it in the resource chapter. Otherwise, be sure to comment on your answers in a journal of some kind.)

Twenty-Seven

Renee: Step Three

A single act of kindness throws out roots in all directions, and the roots spring up and make new trees. — Amelia Earhart

Renee wanted to answer that it was everyone else's fault that she was unhappy. She could prove it, too. The daily news was terrible. The work that she was doing was not satisfying.

She didn't feel appreciated by anyone, and more than one person she worked with picked on her. Plus, she was sure that people laughed at her behind her back because she didn't always understand what they wanted from her.

She didn't like her neighbors either. She thought they were all judging her.

All of it made her think she should move. She could get a new job and find another, more welcoming, place to live. After all, this happiness step was to move yourself if necessary.

Which meant she had to ask herself if it was necessary. What if she was the cause of it all? What if everything she thought was wrong started with her perception of the people, places, and things around her?

Was it their fault she was unhappy? Could she choose to be happy now? Would it make a difference?

Renee took out the list she had started about what made her happy. It wasn't very long. How could so few things make her happy?

Perhaps much of her unhappiness stemmed from not knowing who she was or what she wanted to do with her life. And as hard as she thought about it now, there was nothing in her head about what that could be.

So even if it would be a good idea to move herself, where would she go? If she didn't know what made her happy, how could she make the right choice?

Yes, she told herself. *I am in an abusive situation. But it's not someone else that's doing it. It's me that's doing it to myself.*

Taking out her workbook, Renee started answering all the questions. At first, she judged her answers and got stuck.

Then she decided to set aside the judgment and just write what came to mind. Perhaps something in that stream of consciousness would lead her to what her perfectly blooming life would look and feel like.

In the meantime, she would think like the sunflower. Yes, she was buried behind other plants and sitting in a pile of weeds, but she could still enjoy being herself.

Renee started laughing at that idea. Enjoy being herself? That was a novel idea. It would be interesting to observe, not judge, what grew out of that point of view.

If, after getting to know herself, and observing her interactions with people, showed her it was time to move, at least she'd have a better idea about where to go from there.

Step Four: Feed Yourself The Best Food Possible

Twenty-Eight

We Are What We Eat

Every one of us needs to show how much we care for each other and, in the process, care for ourselves. — Princess Diana

We cheat ourselves by cutting corners and choosing quantity instead of quality. We have grown into a "making it easy and having a lot" society. The result is we put minimal effort into the initial stages of projects, which means we must put a massive effort later into fixing it.

Let's go back to gardening. If we put a plant in poor soil because "who has the time to get that right, besides what difference will that make," and then not water it or feed it, can we expect our plants to grow well, if at all?

Yet, that is our habit in today's society.

Yes, I can be literal and say feed yourself with the best food possible, and we may all stop eating so much nutritionally useless food. I didn't say none of it, but for sure, less of it.

But food means more than literal food. What about what we think about, study, read, watch, spend time on, and hang out with. What about that food?

All plants have different kinds of soil in which they grow best. When we fertilize them, we pick the type that matches who they are. The same applies to our food and how we "eat" it. We are each individual, and we know what is best for us within ourselves. We just don't trust ourselves to listen and act on that wise little voice within.

Let's go back to the idea of perception. My "signature" statement is what you have heard throughout this book—*what you perceive to be reality magnifies.*

This is absolutely true. There is no wiggle room. It has a GOD: *Guarantee Of Delivery.*

It makes sense then to make paying attention to our perceptions a priority. What are they? How are they formed?

We formed many of our perceptions unconsciously. We "inherited" them from parents, the environment, school, and things that happen to us. A soup can fell on our heads when we were three, and we hate soup forever after. That perception shuts the door on any other information about soup, cans, doors opening, and things following.

We have to choose to be conscious, become aware, and be willing to shift our unaware, false, and limiting perceptions and let go of anything that isn't fitting into the infinite perception—my choice and hopefully yours—that good is omnipotent and omnipresent.

When we eat junk perception food, digest it, and hang on to it, we are not building that cool, "I can be happy" perception. We are feeding ourselves small r reality junk perceptions, and then, it's true, "we are what we eat."

What we *perceive—eat—to be reality magnifies* and becomes the life we experience.

Feed yourself the best perceptions you can find. Keep upgrading. This kind of food costs nothing except letting go of false ideas about who you are, which is actually a freedom and not a cost.

Twenty-Nine

Consciously Choose Happiness

The smallest fact is a window through which the infinite may be seen. — Aldous Huxley

In *step three*, we asked ourselves, "Whose fault is it that I am unhappy? Why? And is that true?"

We often feel as if someone or something else has done something that has caused us to be unhappy.

We can be unhappy because of our jobs, income, parents, spouses, children, living conditions, health issues, too much or too little money, governments, terrorists, mosquitoes, too hot or too cold—okay, you and I know I could go on with this list forever.

Nevertheless, doesn't everyone face most of these issues at one time or another, and yet some people are always happy, anyway?

So if we have to assign fault to anyone, it really must come back to us.

This is actually good news because it makes it easier to be happy since we don't have to fix anyone or anything else.

All we have to do is shift our own perception to an awareness and acceptance of happiness. It sounds easy enough, but we all have experienced times when happiness felt entirely out of our reach. Times when we have felt so unhappy, we couldn't remember what makes us happy.

This is where a happiness list of why and what makes us happy comes in handy.

I made my first list one day when I was sitting in a cafe and realized that I was happy for the first time in weeks.

I grabbed a piece of paper and a pen and started writing what made me happy so that if I forgot, I could get out that list and remember.

There were simple things on that list, starting with sitting in a good cafe by myself, and then I added reading a good book, going to the movies, getting a child to smile at me, etc.

None of what was on that first list and following lists were "profound." They were all simple activities. I kept that list, and every time I felt unhappy, I did something on the list. It always worked.

As I expanded my awareness of the quality of happiness, I rarely needed to look at the list anymore, but it was a great place to start.

Once upon a time, when women were birds,
there was the simple understanding that
to sing at dawn and to sing at dusk
was to heal the world through joy.
The birds still remember
what we have forgotten,
that the world is meant to be
celebrated. — Terry Tempest Williams

Thirty

Happy To Want Less

Simplicity of life, even the barest, is not a misery, but the very foundation of refinement. — William Morris

Once upon a time, a coach I was working with told me I could be another Tony Robbins.

I said no. I had no desire to be the person I would have to become to do that.

He didn't understand, and not long after that told me he couldn't work with me anymore. Well, his actual words were he couldn't help me anymore.

I suppose, in his mind, I was beyond help.

But it wasn't that. What he wanted for me, I didn't want for myself. And not for one second have I ever regretted that decision. But what did I want?

Less. And more.

Less need. More grace.

Having worked in the financial industry for years, I knew that all the money in the world, the biggest house, the biggest company, couldn't buy grace. Didn't bring happiness.

We find grace and happiness elsewhere. And once found, wealth doesn't rob us of them; it serves them.

As the world is in reset mode and people decide whether kindness is more important than winning, most of us are also resetting our wants, needs, and priorities.

But, when it is all over, what will we go back to? Do we have to choose overwhelm?

For me, in that moment when I said no, I decided to want less and be happier. But I still constantly re-examine exactly what that means for me.

It doesn't mean I don't plan on doing more. Happiness and expansion are not exclusive. It's how it's done.

Expansion and sharing are the essences of life. From the expansion of the universe to the continual growth of a forest, we understand that to be true. All life expands. But nothing in nature does it by itself. Each element intertwines within the whole.

All our lives are also intertwined. My need can not override yours. My expansion can not destroy yours. And the way we each expand is personal and uniquely individual.

I expand and share as a turtle, and I am happy to be one.

Every day I write a little of the next book. Edit the one I just finished. Record the audio of the book before that. Edit that recording. Learn something new. Spend time on ads and marketing. Coach. Teach classes. Work on websites and merchandise.

And I also work in the garden, walk, do yoga and pilates, make a meal or two, read, watch TV, talk to Del, check in with family.

Step by step, plodding along. Wanting less, being more happy. But still with big dreams about what I want to do in life.

Nelson Mandela said, *It always seems impossible until it's done.*

It's all about intent. The goal and the to-do list follow. They don't drive the action; they are the action.

Did I want to be the next Tony Robbins? No.

But I did, and do, want to shift people's perceptions and lives towards the infinite. That's my intent. That's my mission. That's the dream I follow. How big or small that becomes is not what is essential.

Doing it well is.

We don't have to choose overwhelm. We can walk away from it. We can want less. And still do more—in our own way.

Be the next Tony Robbins, or Oprah, or Steve Jobs, if that is your calling. I'll be rooting for you. But do it your way and don't give up the essence of your life to do it. It won't be worth the price.

And every day, each of us has to ask ourselves the same question. "What is more important in this moment, and will it be kind and helpful to others?"

If we do that, we may find ourselves in that state of mind called heaven on earth. And really, what could be more important than that?

Thirty-One

Choose Consciously

*C**hildren have never been very good at listening to their elders, but they have never failed to imitate them.* — James Baldwin

Part of choosing consciously is becoming aware of what we have already chosen or accepted as our choice when it really isn't. Either it's come from a worldview, or from a local view, like parents, teachers, friends, and trying to fit it.

Eventually, we need to make our own choices to live as our unique spiritual blessings. Design our own perceptions and choose our own point of view and state of mind.

This is a simple exercise to help you do that. I use I Choose sheets in every class and mention them in almost every book in *The Shift Series*. Why? Because doing them makes an enormous difference. They don't take much work. It is not necessary to study them, keep them around, or worry about them. Just do them. And then let go.

This is what that looks like taken from the book *Perception Mastery*.

I choose, therefore I am. — Amit Goswami

Did you know there's a voice in your head constantly telling you why you can't do something? This voice is called many things: the monkey voice, the ego, the shadow—whatever you call it, it's imperative to know and understand one thing. That voice is not your voice. I know it sounds like you, and it says things you think you might say to yourself, but it's not.

So, why is it there?

That's like asking why do we believe we are human. Who knows? At this point, it's all someone's story. Believe them or not, it changes nothing.

Here's what we do know, and it does change things. The voice in our head runs the paradigm we think we must live within, and unless we know what it is saying to us, we are stuck in its prison. It drives the car we call our life. It has us choosing things we may or may not want anymore, or perhaps never wanted.

However, we have free will, so let's put that freedom to work.

Let's find out what that voice is saying and then replace it with what we consciously choose. Being willing, becoming aware, and consciously choosing breaks open our current paradigm. It shifts our perception. And as a result, the world we experience shifts to match our new perception.

Remember, perception is reality. *What we perceive to be reality magnifies.*

Therefore, since we can make conscious choices, let's shift our perception to the best version of what I call big R Reality that we can get to right now. Which, for me, and perhaps for you, is a gloriously Loving One Intelligent Reality, because that's the one I want to experience.

Now that we know what we would consciously choose, let's do an I Choose sheet. Doing this is so simple it might seem ineffective. However, I promise you it works if you do it.

Here we go:
Get out a tablet of paper and a pen. Notice I didn't say get your computer. I love writing on my computer. But I Choose sheets work much better when they are handwritten. Besides, when you finish with one, you can burn it. Very satisfying. Or write in a tablet and then clear the page when you are finished.

Begin by stating what you want as a choice.
How do you know what you want? Look back in this book and choose one of the things that makes you happy.

After that, there are just two steps to learn.

- First, pause, and listen for the voice in your head telling you why you can't have it or why it won't work.

I guarantee you that the voice is there. Don't worry. It can't hurt to hear it now. In fact, you want to listen to what it's been telling you all along, and you have been accepting as true.

Once you hear that voice telling you why you can't have what you want, don't write what that voice says. Please don't give it any power by agreeing with it.

- Next, choose and write the opposite of what it's saying. I call this "face and replace."

Face what it says, and replace it with what you consciously choose.

That's it ... just keep going until there is nothing left to face and replace. It may take pages and pages. After you are done, there is no need to keep the pages around!

Thirty-Two

Practical Blooming: Step Four

Perfection is like chasing the horizon. Keep moving. — Neil Gaiman

Think of this as a clearing out of your closets and cupboards. Just as you might say, I don't eat this anymore, or I don't wear this anymore. This is an "I don't think or live this anymore" cleaning out.

If you aren't sure you don't want it, go ahead and keep it. But put it aside to be examined later. Don't put the cans of food, the clothes, or old perceptions back in the same place. Store them somewhere you can observe them after some time has passed.

Make your life an endless series of "Spring Cleaning," and let go of what is not working.

Think of it as a gift to yourself, and have fun. Please do your best to enjoy the mess it might make at first, knowing that everything will feel better once it's done.

1. I notice that I have "inherited" these perceptions.
2. Observing my life, I see I have these unconscious perceptions.
3. I realize I am carrying these perceptions from my past.
4. I am willing to choose my own perceptions. Yes - Not Sure - No

5. I am willing to let go of any perception that does not bloom in my life. Yes - Not Sure - No
6. I choose this point of view perception.
7. I choose to remain in this state of mind perception.
8. This is what makes me happy.
9. Do an I Choose sheet on at least one thing that makes you happy.

Things to do as you make your happiness list:

- See yourself as happy.

- What are you doing?

- What are you thinking?

- Take notes, so you remember.

Thank you for taking this time for yourself. This is feeding yourself the kind of food that will radically change your life.

Once you have answered the questions in your workbook, join me in the next step.

I'll be sitting on my bench under the apple tree, listening to the music and rhythms of nature, and waiting to walk the garden with you.

Thirty-Three

Renee: Step Four

All God's angels come to us disguised. — James Russell Lowell

As Renee built her list of things that made her happy, she decided to try a little experiment with her neighbors. Instead of trying to ignore them because she knew they didn't like her, she waved and smiled at them. A part of her got a kick out of it, thinking that if they didn't like her, that would make them anxious, wondering what she was up to.

But she recognized that was just another version of her thinking the world was against her and did her best to let that thought go, and instead chose the POV that cooperation and community existed in her world.

What surprised her was that because her neighbor smiled and waved back, it made it onto her happiness list.

That gave her the impetus to choose to see herself as happy and act as if she was, even if she wasn't. She realized that what she told herself or allowed herself to believe that was negative about people, places, and things didn't give her impetus to change. It only increased her feelings of isolation and unhappiness. She decided they were junk food thoughts.

That day she ran across Albert Einstein's quote, *The ideals which have lighted my way, and time after time have given me new courage to face life cheerfully, have been Kindness, Beauty, and Truth*, and realized those were good food thoughts. She could choose them for herself and see what happened.

Renee still wasn't sure if she needed to move, change jobs, or change homes, but she knew she needed to be healthier in her thinking. She wasn't living in a dangerous situation. Her work was okay, so it was safe to take the time to think and eat better first. For that, she was grateful.

That night, she started writing out what she imagined her perfect life would look like and feel like. She had so few ideas she had to use bits from books and movies to make it up. Renee was sure it wasn't what she really wanted, but she had to start somewhere.

Over time, she could rewrite the story as she got to know herself better. And whatever the voice in her head was trying to tell her, she would tell it to shush. She was done thinking it was telling her the truth. Renee decided to trust her still small voice within instead. The one she hadn't been listening to for a long time, but she could start now.

That thought made her happy. She added it to her happiness list.

STEP FIVE: GROW IN YOUR OWN TIMING

Thirty-Four

Your Timing Is Perfect

I am not a complainer. If I was that type of person, I would be cluttering the path that God has laid out for me, and I wouldn't be able to walk it. — Regina King

Sometimes we are happy, but we act unhappy and don't realize it.

I had a vivacious grandmother who was a lover of life. However, she constantly complained under her breath. I am sure she didn't know she was doing it.

I have a clear memory of her looking under the sink, trying to get something out and the running commentary of her complaining while she was doing it. I do that same thing sometimes. When I am observing myself, I am amazed that it is happening.

She was happy. I am happy. However, if you heard that complaining, would you know?

Family habits! We can dissolve them!

When we complain, either consciously or unconsciously, we reinforce the human-computer program that produces what we perceive as our life.

This program doesn't know that we are happy; it doesn't know we don't mean what we are complaining about.

It hears unhappiness and assumes that is what we want more of, and so it shrinks our perception down to what it thinks we believe, actually reducing the possibilities of our lives.

Or, said more simply: *What we perceive to be reality magnifies.*

It's up to us to choose a different reality.

I know you either want to, or already have, chosen the point of view of the big r Reality of Infinite Mind. However, the crucial step is to live in big r Reality by consciously choosing the state of mind that reinforces this point of view.

Consciously choose happiness, consciously stay in the state of mind of happiness, and it will reveal what is already true—that happiness exists because divine Love is.

To help us get to, and stay in, this state of mind, our new habit will be to observe happiness and trust ourselves to see it.

Spend the time to grow a strong root structure.

No matter how quickly or slowly you are doing the work in this book, you may become impatient with the "outside" results.

So let's talk more about being kind to yourself and trusting in your timing.

I thought about these seven simple steps after observing some Narcissus bulbs that I was forcing into bloom so that we could enjoy their beauty along with the snow falling outside.

One year, I put the bulbs in different glass containers on top of rocks, added water, and placed them around our combo kitchen-living room, which is full of light.

Although they all experienced the same conditions, something strange happened.

Within days, one bulb started sending out roots, and the others just sat there. Nothing, nada. I waited for over a week, thinking that they were just different, but still nothing.

Then I started wondering what was different about their living conditions that could cause the delay.

After much pondering, I realized the simple answer was their containers. The bulb that had developed roots was sitting in a fairly shallow container. The others were in a deep one because I thought it would be beautiful to see them grow though the glass.

Do you see what the problem was? It took me a while to figure it out, but then I realized they were getting different amounts of oxygen.

I took all the bulbs out of the deep container and put them all in shallower ones. Within a day, one of them had sent out its roots.

But not all. It took weeks for some of them to grow again after their not-so-perfect first place planting. This goes back to the step - Plant Yourself Where You Grow Best.

Another interesting thing happened. One bulb grew and then bloomed even faster than the first bulb, which had the few weeks' head start.

I love to grow these bulbs in glass containers because it makes it possible to see their beautiful root system. One little root reaches out and touches the water. Discovering support, it is quickly joined by other roots growing so fast you can almost see it happening.

They spread out into the rocks and water to support the growth that is happening above. The leaves and the bloom are the "payoff," but without that root system, they could not grow at all.

Here's what this is all about to me: blooming lives, or not blooming lives.

For each of us to bloom, it is always important to notice where we are planted and decide if we are getting enough "oxygen."

The bulbs needed me to notice their situation and move them. We can not only notice what we need, but move ourselves to a better place to bloom.

We also need deep roots to grow and bloom well and long. Sometimes we question if our lives will ever bloom and forget to notice the beautiful growth of our roots beneath the surface, preparing to support what will become visible.

During a cold snap, the plants that were growing rapidly stopped growing. At least on the surface. They were increasing their root system while they waited for the warm weather to return.

Timing is different for each of us. Some of us are fast growers, but slow bloomers. Others are slow growers, but speedy bloomers.

However, what is true about each of us is that when we give ourselves the support, patience, and substance necessary to bloom, we will bloom—in our own timing.

There is a worldview that if we haven't reached our full potential or bloomed by a certain age, we haven't succeeded. This false perception starts early in life.

We are supposed to talk by a certain age, write by a certain age, speak by a certain age, date, get married by a certain age, have babies, buy a house, and be successful—all by a certain age. The idea of specific blooming periods is all timed out and predetermined by an arbitrary scale, none of which is true or relates to our USB and finding our path.

I always have to stifle a giggle when I hear a teenager or someone in their twenties lamenting that they do not know what they are supposed to be when they grow up.

Be? By that, they mean to be successful at something which we often determine based on the erroneous measurement of money.

What if we measured success by how happy we are? Would there be a time requirement for that? Could money measure it? No!

Although money is a good thing and makes life easier, it is not the source of our happiness.

For most of us, we are too busy doing the outside work of growing branches and leaves that we never take the time to put down deep roots into the soil of our unique self. A self that will absolutely bloom in its proper season if we have given ourselves the time and attention we deserve.

We will also bloom repeatedly. It's not a onetime thing. Each season of life produces unique blooms.

This all goes back to the concept of knowing who you are, valuing it, and following all the steps that we have talked about in this book.

As I write this book, it's spring and I have seeds growing in my kitchen waiting for warmer weather. They are happy sitting on warming pads with a light hanging above them.

My husband and I love stopping by a few times a day to check what has popped out of the ground. And yes, we both talk to them, encouraging them along, telling them how happy we are to see them grow.

Watching the birth of these plants always reminds me that ideas are like that. Some come up right away, bursting out of the ground loudly, others wait and we have to look closely to see that they are there.

Give your ideas water, warmth, light, food... and then... like plants, most of them will grow. You can thin them out later—choosing the ones that will grow best.

Every seed has everything in it that it needs to grow. The same thing is true for each of us.

Be patient, tender, kind, and loving to yourself. Pay attention to what you need, and make sure you provide it. Each step in this process will bring you more ideas and inspiration.

And perhaps, spend a little time thinking about the happiest person you know. Why are they? Perhaps ask them. And if you answer that you are, celebrate that fact. If that's not true yet, keep growing. It will be.

Thirty-Five

What The Past Reveals

*H*ofstadter's Law: It always takes longer than you expect, even when you take into account Hofstadter's Law. — Douglas Hofstadter

All winter, the blue storage box sat alone on the garage floor, calling me.

Years before, my husband and I had left it with my daughter for safekeeping on our way to more traveling. When we finished traveling, she returned it, but I didn't open it, knowing it would require something from me I didn't feel ready to do—face all those memories from the past.

Finally, on a beautiful spring day, I opened the blue box. Out came yearbooks, a bunch of videos—destined to be converted to DVDs after tearful watching—my dance thesis, and a gaggle of picture albums.

Underneath all that, I glimpsed the scrapbook that I had once treasured and had thought I had lost. It was a treasure trove of myself from the past. On the first page, I found something I had saved from when I had just graduated from college and, along with my children, was headed off into a new adventure. I was leaving the dance world (mostly) behind and heading into the business world. Scared and excited, but willing.

Also on that first page was a poem by Victor Hugo that I have carried with me for years. And there was a note from my now-grown daughter, written in 5th grade, promising me she would not give me any trouble when she was a teenager. I laughed—happy that she now has her own daughter—and that she had kept her promise the best that any teenager could.

However, the treasure that filled most of the pages were essays from my favorite writers, cut out of magazines and newspapers. They fueled my childhood desire to write and move people the same way those writers moved me.

I read one. It was even better than I remembered. I had to stop looking through the scrapbook for a few days because I was so overwhelmed with the happiness of this discovery.

The scrapbook contains many inspirations that helped me develop my first class on perception, first called *The Power Of Perception* and then *The Shift*, that I began teaching in 1992. Later, I wrote a book based on what I learned teaching that class, and I added those ideas to the scrapbook. I could see little notes to myself telling me on which page of the first draft of the book I had used specific quotes.

The length of time between each of those memories proves to me, once again, that life isn't a disconnected series of events, but it expands as a complete unit, each spiral adding deeper and higher meanings to every event.

It reminds me of our garden. Each year we add more nutrients to the soil, and each year it is a richer environment in which seeds can grow.

Our lives are like that too.

What I was as a child is still here with me now as a grandmother; just more of it, deeper and richer. What I wanted to do, what I believed in then, and wanted to be, is still present, and the scrapbook is my witness.

That book, which first came from the scrapbook, is *Living In Grace: The Shift To Spiritual Perception*. I developed it from a lifetime of observation, listening, and collecting ideas, as contained in that scrapbook, plus much more.

When I finished that book, I thought I had done my job, and that was all the writing I was going to do. Of course, now I know it was only the beginning.

Sometimes it helps to look back and see how the events in our lives unfolded because it helps us remember that we can trust that our lives, properly tended and cared for, unfolds in its own timing bringing even more extraordinary beauty as what we call time moves on.

> *Be like the bird, who*
> *Halting in his flight*
> *On limb too slight*
> *Feels it give way beneath him,*
> *Yet sings*
> *Knowing he hath wings.* — Victor Hugo

Thirty-Six

Live Your Why

To laugh often and much; to win the respect of the intelligent people and the affection of children; to earn the appreciation of honest critics and endure the betrayal of false friends; to appreciate beauty; to find the beauty in others; to leave the world a bit better whether by a healthy child, a garden patch, or a redeemed social condition; to know that one life has breathed easier because you lived here. This is to have succeeded. — Ralph Waldo Emerson

The end of this quote has always struck me as the perfect why of being alive. To know even one life has breathed easier because you have lived. This is to have succeeded.

How simple this would make all our decisions if we followed this idea. And although each of us achieves this in our unique way, it can be the perfect "why" for each of us.

However, "the what-or the what's in it for me point of view," is celebrated instead. Get rich, get famous, get, and more get. This is the false manhood come into power, unchecked by true womanhood. It's going after that "what" and not following the "why."

The why, asks us to consider the underlying reason for our sharing our days with each other. What do we most bring into life that means something? What differences do we, and can we, make?

In 1964, Bob Dylan wrote, "The times they are a changing."

As we change, let's make sure that we move away from a false sense of male as conqueror and controller, and into both the true sense of manhood as protector, and action taker, and true womanhood as the guide to wise action.

Let's move into choosing the why as the motivator, not the what.

I am a lover of all design shows. I love watching the design unfold and the contestants find themselves and become more of their unique spiritual blessing. However, sometimes they lose their way. On a fashion design show a few years ago, an additional $10,000 cash prize was announced for the winner of the week's competition.

At which point, one woman in the competition, who previously had done well, stopped being able to create anything. She cried, and worried, and blamed others, and couldn't stop thinking about how much she needed the money.

She had turned into wanting something and completely forgot her why. Her creation, and the process of creating it, was a disaster.

Remembering, and expressing, our why, and not getting caught up in the temptation of the what is a practice. We admire people that don't forget their why. Perhaps we don't always agree, or like what they do, but we admire their clarity and honesty.

The vehicle of expression is not the important part, it's knowing, and expressing, the why that is important.

I watched our family move another member of the family into their new home. I witnessed how each member easily and gracefully worked their why throughout the day, and no one said what's in it for me.

Doors were removed so a refrigerator could come through, plumbing was fixed, new locks were installed, cleaning took place, clothes put away, and beds made so that sleep was possible at the end of the day. Everyone did their part, without division, as one unit working in harmony.

Imagine this happening everywhere, all the time—everyone choosing to make someone else's life easier!

Let's make sure that all our changes are being fully directed by our why, and that why is always based on kindness and respect for all living things. When the why, based on each unique expression of the Divine, is the raison d'être, we all thrive and we all find happiness in the process.

Thirty-Seven

Practical Blooming: Step Five

Thank you all for being such faithful tenders of your garden. We are preparing for an abundant harvest, now, and far into the future.

As you answer these questions, think about walking to the open door that has always been there for you. The one that calls to you with love and abundance. Let yourself move to that door. You will know that you are moving towards it by the joy you feel rising in your life.

When you are ready, I will be waiting for you in the garden.

1. What did I learn from my past?
2. How is what I learned nourishing my life now?
3. Where are my current roots?
4. How deep are they?
6. Am I allowing the roots to go deep?
7. Am I rushing the process? Yes - Not Sure - No
9. What ideas am I currently growing?

Thirty-Eight

Renee: Step Five

Happiness is not a matter of intensity, but of balance, order, rhythm, and harmony. —Thomas Merton

The question, *what did I learn from my past*, threw Renee for a loop. If she really answered what she learned from her past, she could answer that question for days. *Besides,* she asked herself, *what is the past? Does it mean yesterday, or when I was two, or before I was born, or maybe just a minute ago?*

All those things were in the past. *Pick one,* she told herself. *Then go pick another.* So she started with what she had learned a minute ago. That she was very analytical, and that wasn't a bad thing. But it could stop her in her tracks by getting stuck on questions that had either no answer or multiple answers.

Good to know, she said to herself. *Use it correctly, so it serves me. Use that skill when it's helpful and let go of it when it isn't.*

Moving back to something she learned from her mother, she realized she used food as a requirement, comfort, and a reward. With that realization, Renee decided to eat the best food possible when she was hungry and not reward herself with it anymore. Or at least notice when she did.

Observe, don't judge, Renee reminded herself. Otherwise, guilt or shame would make her want to eat more to comfort herself, which would only bring her back full circle.

Each time Renee asked herself what she learned from her past, she realized she had a choice of whether or not to keep that perception. And she could change her mind as she evolved in her understanding of herself and what brought her joy.

Bringing herself to the present, Renee wondered what brought her joy because that was where she wanted to spread her roots. She took out her what-makes-me-happy list to find out.

That's when Renee realized there was something not on the list that always used to make her happy. She loved going to classes and doing things that involved creativity.

Wow, Renee said to herself, *I am happy when I create something. And I like being around other people doing the same thing!*

Does it matter what I create, she asked herself. The answer was she didn't know. But she remembered how much she enjoyed going to art class. She'd start there and see where it took her.

Since she remembered that she learned best in groups, Renee found a local art class and signed up. It was a beginning. She had planted a seed, and she expected it to come up in its own timing and in its own way.

STEP SIX: EXPECT TO BLOOM

Thirty-Nine

Yes, It Will Come Up

The future belongs to those who believe in the beauty of their dreams. —Eleanor Roosevelt

It was spring when I first wrote these seven steps of happiness. Although I grew up in Pennsylvania, I lived in California as an adult. Every spring, I would say to my family in the east, "Yes, it is spring here too," and they would smile and say, "Hum."

And now that I am back in the east, I know what they meant. The spring in a place where there has been cold and snow for months arrives with more intensity, and the search for spring is a daily activity.

In February, I look for signs of spring, and I find them. The preamble to the season hides within the cold, but it's there.

However, when true spring arrives, it sweeps in like the wind. One day it is dark and dreary, and the next, the trees are wearing gorgeous halos of red and yellow buds.

The daffodils are not visible one day and nodding their golden heads in the breeze the next. You have to carefully observe each day not to miss spring as it bursts forth from winter.

The harbingers and celebrators of spring are the birds. They sing with every fiber of their being, belting out songs with abandon. They glow with happiness.

Yes, this is all about happiness.

Buried beneath what may appear as a winter of unhappiness are the seeds of happiness—just waiting for the warmth of love to burst forth.

I can see each of you on your tree of life, singing of joy with every fiber of your being.

Before the sun comes up, birds begin their dawn chorus. You can start now, too, knowing that nothing can stop the sun, or your happiness—in its multitudes of forms—from rising and being known.

Because it is always within you.

We contain within ourselves, as the bulb and the acorn contain its substance within, all the elements of a beautiful blooming life. Like the bulb and the acorn, we are designed to grow and bloom into our lives as the Unique Spiritual Blessing that we are.

So what stops the process?

Years ago, I heard a fable that has become a favorite of mine because it illustrates so clearly why we often stop expecting to bloom, and in not expecting to, we do not.

At one time, the devil was said to be going out of business. His tools would be for sale to anyone who would pay his price. On the night of the sale, they were all displayed—malice, envy, hatred, jealousy, sensualism, deceit, and all the other implements of evil.

Separate from the rest lay a harmless-looking, wedge-shaped tool. It was much worn and priced higher than any of the others.

When someone asked the devil what it was, he said, "That's discouragement."

"Well, why do you have it priced so high?"

"Because," answered the devil, "it is more useful to me than any of the others because I can pry open and get inside someone's thought with that when I couldn't touch them in any other way. It is so worn because I use it with nearly everybody, as very few people know that it belongs to me."

"Is there anyone on whom you can't use it?"

The devil hesitated a long time and finally said in a low voice, "I can't use it in a grateful heart."

At the sale, the devil's price for discouragement was so high that it was never sold. The fable concludes, he still owns it, and he is still using it.

When I was a little girl, I had a favorite little book and record that went with it. It was about a boy who had planted some carrot seeds. He waited and waited, but they didn't come up. He expected them to.

However, his brother teased him constantly, saying, "Naw, naw, it won't come up."

How discouraging. This is exactly what the worldview says about living happy lives. "Naw, naw, it won't come up." All the time. It's constant, just like the sibling's constant "Naw, naw, it won't come up."

And since it takes a while for carrot seeds to sprout, it was hard to hold to the fact that they would.

He stared at them every day. Made sure they had the proper soil, light, and water and waited as patiently as he could.

The "Naw, Naw" kept up, and he sometimes rebutted it, sometimes said nothing, but kept on watching for the seeds to sprout.

I have never forgotten that story because of his courage, and vision, and faith. And, of course, those carrots came up. It is within a seed to sprout, and it will when given the right conditions.

There are some other key points here.

The little boy didn't fool around in the soil, checking to see if the seeds had roots. When they began to sprout, he didn't pull them up to see how big the roots were because both actions would have killed this tender sprout.

The same thing is true with ideas. Be careful with whom you share your plans to bloom. Actually, this is one reason we have a thriving *Perception Circle*, a community of like-minded souls shifting from the limited to the unlimited, and is a safe place to share and get help to bloom.

Take care not to worry and fret, which is the same thing as pulling up the roots. Everything that we are talking about, the entire universe of blooming, is happening within.

If fret, worry, doubt, and discouragement are part of your inner world and you haven't yet learned how to shut it down, dissolve it, watch it float by, or at least stop believing it, you will struggle instead of thriving.

It is within you to bloom, given the right conditions. The good news is that these right conditions are all within you now. You have a right to change what everyone else might say are the rules and be happy.

Plants in the wrong situation can't move by themselves.

But we can, and in a very real sense, we must so that others can thrive too.

Without every bulb blooming, the complete picture of the garden is not present. Following this metaphor, each of us blooming is necessary for the garden called God—or Infinite Intelligence, or Divine Order, or Love—to be seen and experienced.

Sometimes, what seems complicated is actually quite simple. These seven steps help us see and live that simplicity.

Can you feel the quality of ease present within the seven steps? Happiness is already present within you. We are shifting our perception to this fact and taking steps to reveal it.

After Will Smith's now-famous misbehavior at the 2022 Oscars, Denzel Washington reminded him that, "At your highest moment, be careful. That's when the devil comes for you."

But that pull to bring us down also happens at our lowest moments.

Being happy for no good reason is a great defense against the "devil."

Choose happiness, my friends. It's an open door to the Divine, the Universe of Infinite Intelligence and Love.

Forty

Designed To Be Filled

The rain begins with a single drop. — Manal al-Sharif

Have you ever stood in an empty football stadium? The experience of standing in that open space is awe-inspiring. It's a space just waiting to be filled. It's a space that understands its purpose and is perfectly designed to fulfill that purpose.

I had this experience during a high school reunion when we visited the Penn State University football stadium. We took the elevators that are accessed only by a special key to the top level, and stepped out into the empty, light-filled stadium.

Our tour guide shared the history of the stadium's expansion. He took us from its beginning and its move to the present location. Throughout the years, the stadium has expanded in progressive steps, always improving.

It continues its purpose, to provide a space for many people to bring their hopes and dreams, and to make memories. Each step of its expansion has cost time and money, and has involved collaboration between a wide diversity of people and talents.

Instead of closing down and doing less as time moved on, the stadium has expanded and accepted new ideas, providing more space to be filled with the qualities of joy, happiness, expectation, intent, and celebration.

As I stood in that empty stadium and listened to the tour guide, I felt the correlation of the stadium to the way we live our lives. Like the stadium, our lives are also a space designed to be filled. But, unlike the stadium, we are not always clear about our purpose, or willing to fulfill it.

As time moves on, we are often tempted to do less. We stay stuck, or comfortable, in our patterns of beliefs and judgments. But like the stadium, our lives are designed to be filled with ideas, hopes, love, joy, happiness, compassion, intents, caring, gifts, memories, people, and celebration.

Being exclusionary, and shutting down, is counter to our purpose.

Recently, two new digital boards were added to the PSU stadium. This new technology will enable everyone in the stadium to see a clear picture of what is happening on the field. The stadium continues to move with the times, with a cost of time, money, and patience and with a strong willingness to go forward into the future.

Do we do the same? Do we allow our lives to grow and expand so that we can be more of what we have been designed to be? Although our lives are designed to be filled, we are responsible for the expansion that enables that to happen.

As in all things, size doesn't matter. Some people's lives are as full as a stadium; others are smaller and more intimate. But, in all cases, we are the ones who must be willing to expand to allow more ideas and people into our lives. It takes work. Sometimes it takes money. It always takes patience.

However, that has always been our purpose, and in the end, it is what blooms our lives in joy, and where we find fulfillment. Yes, we are designed to be filled with happiness.

Forty-One

Let Go and Rise

*F*or *he shall give his angels charge over thee, to keep thee in all thy ways.* — Psalm 91:11

One spring, I hung a suet feeder on a branch of a tree right outside my office. I hung it there because it was visible as I worked at my computer. It was delightful to have the company of birds like woodpeckers, blue jays, nuthatches, titmice, chickadees, and cardinals as they pecked away at the suet.

When I needed to fill the feeder, I would grab a lower branch, pull it toward me and bounce it. That would bring down the branch with the feeder to my level.

As fall approached, I noticed something I had never realized before, but seems perfectly obvious in hindsight. Did you know that as leaves drop off branches, the branches rise? Not just a few inches, they really rise.

One night, as I took the feeder off a branch that had dropped its leaves, it popped back into the air at least five feet. I laughed in delight at my discovery, and in the realization that I would have to find another way to grab the branch!

My imagination took off as I thought of how the tree must feel to be free and clean to begin again, to be able to lift itself up higher into the sunlight. As the trees let go, the display of beautiful color and raining leaves is stunning. It's not a sad time, it is a season of harvest and abundance and rising!

We, on the other hand, tend to hold on to what is over, or is no longer useful. In fact, not only do we hoard, we gather what we don't need, just in case we need it someday.

Imagine trees acting like us, keeping their dead leaves, and then growing new ones, keeping them when they die, growing more, and keeping them, too.

As the cycle continued, instead of rising, the branch would droop lower and lower until eventually the weight of it all would bring it down. Or what if the tree let the leaves go, but then gathered them up, and tried to reattach them to themselves?

The trees, knowing that all that it needs is within and will create anew, releases, and rises, and restores, and glories in its freedom. Each tree has its own timing when and how it lets go, but it always does. As it lets go, it reveals its true structure, its limbs tracing beautiful shapes in the air and sky.

We are afraid that we are not like the tree, with all that we need already contained within our true nature. So we hold on to beliefs, ideas, and decisions that weigh us down, until one day we break under their weight, or simply stop growing exhausted from the effort of holding on.

Every leaf that dropped off the tree branch made a difference in how high the branch would rise. I could see the branch lift a little more each day. Just a light little leaf, one at a time, makes a difference, and once they were all gone, the branch leapt into the air!

Sometimes we may feel discouraged that all we can do is let go of little things, like a small unwelcome belief, a tiny fault forgiven, a false memory dissolved. Perhaps we think that we have to do big things to make a difference. Each leaf says otherwise.

In our fireplace, the logs were carefully placed, but not burning. Deep underneath them, I glimpsed a small red core, so tiny it was hardly visible. As I watched, within minutes, the fire exploded into action; the flames leaping up to the ceiling of the stove.

We might only have a small deep core within that is holding to what is true and beautiful, and perhaps it feels as if we have been doing that forever and yet nothing has happened. The fire says otherwise.

Life is about the little things. Each moment gives us something to affirm as Truth, or to let go of because it's no longer needed or wanted.

All that we see and know gives us a message. Everything that we experience is a symbol, not a thing. Whether it is a person, a spark, or a leaf, it is a symbol of the qualities that make up its true substance.

As we understand this idea, it becomes easier to let go and rise and feel the freedom of knowing that all that we are contains all that we need in every moment. Feeding the fire of this knowledge, the core of our being warms and then leaps into action, and that benefits not only ourselves but also those whose lives we touch.

So go ahead, let go, rise and enjoy the lightness of being, the sunlight of love, and the comforting warmth of the knowledge that you are the idea of Divine Love and therefore always and eternally safe and free.

Forty-Two

The Qualities Of What We Desire

A bird does not sing because it has an answer. It sings because it has a song. — Chinese Proverb

No book in *The Shift Series* would be complete without talking about why and how to use quality words. In this book, our focus is on blooming our lives. To what end, though?

As you take yourself through these seven steps intending to bloom, hopefully there will be things you want to change, places you want to go, and things you desire.

All of which is part of the process of blooming. The problem lies in that although we may believe that we do—we don't really know what we want. We have a picture in our head about it, a story that we have told ourselves. Outside forces, or internal patterns and habits, perceptions, that we accepted as truth, have influenced and driven that picture and story, and although they once were useful, they no longer serve us.

For example: We may decide we want a red car, go out and buy one, but it never satisfies the actual need. If you examine your life and often find a sense of dissatisfaction, one reason may be that you went after the thing, and not the idea. Or qualities.

But what are qualities? They are what makes up a thing, or idea. One way to say it is they are not nouns. They are describers.

Sometimes we make a quality word list on how something would look. Sometimes we make a quality word list on how something would feel if we were doing it, or had it. But we use describers not nouns.

Remember, we talked about POV and SOM perceptions? Making a feeling quality word list brings our state of mind into harmony with our point of view.

Using the car example. Let's say we realize we need a better way to get ourselves from here to there. Instead of saying we want a red car, we say something like this: "I desire transportation."

This statement is shorthand for all that lies behind it. But you, as the writer, would have all the feelings and needs internally, so it's just a holding place and symbol of all that you mean by it.

Now. Instead of stating a noun, describe first how you would feel if you had the perfect transportation for yourself.

Maybe your list would include safe, secure, easy, clean, comfortable, and quick. Notice that these are simple descriptors and not nouns.

What may happen after making this list is you realize this is not a car. It's a bike, a bus, a train, walking, or riding with a friend.

But, let's assume you decide it is a car. Perhaps then you could make a list of what it would look like. No nouns, though. However, when I make a list like this for a car, it's usually very short. The last list went something like this: not red, white or black. Heated seats. Rated high in safety. Good mileage. Room to carry things.

But first, it had to satisfy how I would feel: safe, secure, comfortable. Notice safe was on my list twice. So when I researched my car, I checked how high its safety rating was first, and everything else fell into place.

If you are not in the habit of doing quality word lists before you get or do anything major (or even small things) I hope you will take up the practice. Life will become much more satisfying and you will find that doing all seven steps of Blooming Your Life much easier.

Forty-Three

Quality Word Details

*H*appiness *is when what you think, what you say, and what you do are in harmony.* — Mahatma Gandhi

Going back to the car example, here's an excerpt from the book From *Living In Grace* that explains more about how to do and use Quality word lists.

You will notice that you need someone else to help you put the Quality word lists in order. And they **do** need to be put into order. Otherwise, they are in the order of how your intellectual mind thinks they should be and not your heart. And that means you will still end up with something that will not satisfy what you want.

You will find more instructions, including visual instructions, and an ongoing community of people that are always available to order a list in the resource chapter of this book.

Or find a friend and do this together!

From *Living In Grace: The Shift To Spiritual Perception*
Turning things into thoughts.

Pick anything that you're thinking about, or desiring to see, and list its qualities. For example, let's say that you were thinking about a car. You want the idea or quality of transportation. So how would you like that transportation to look? You might say that its qualities include safety, effortlessness, speed, security, luxury, grace, convenience, and so on.

You have probably phrased this request as something you want or need. However, if you use the words "need" or "want," they imply that you're lacking something. It is a statement of separation. As an expression or reflection of the Infinite One Loving Mind, how could you lack? If you believe you are lacking, you are.

What we perceive to be reality magnifies, so if we perceive lack, we receive lack. An unlimited Reality cannot lack; therefore, neither can you.

You have never been separated from God. In addition, wanting something often involves our ego, or human will asking for it. When we use human will, or ego, we are walking the mental or physical path. We think we are the cause and creator. We believe that if we do enough, know enough, or work hard enough, we can fix the problem. This is not putting God First. It is putting "me first." To avoid this trap of personal ego, which blinds us to the will of God, we ask instead "to see." Since everything has already been created, we are asking ourselves to wake up to what has already been provided.

Steps to making qualities lists.

Remember again, we are not interested in things here. We are interested in knowing God. Since things are in essence composed of qualities, we translate back into qualities the things of which we desire to become conscious.

Step 1: Take a moment and list 8–10 qualities of something you want to experience. Use one word to express each quality. If you are using sentences, you have not come to the heart or essence of it.

Step 2: There are two kinds of qualities lists: You can either list the qualities of the thing itself, or you can list the qualities of how you will feel when you have it.

For example, let's go back to the idea of buying a car. Your quality list for the thing—or car—might contain ideas such as red, fast, inexpensive, safe, etc.

If you choose to do a qualities list of how you will feel when you drive this car, it might read "wealthy, secure, free, joyful, etc."

If you wish, do both lists. Otherwise, do the list that makes the most sense to you. What you choose to see does not matter. It can be as important as having a home or as simple as setting the table for dinner. It is being conscious of the qualities of these "things" that makes a difference.

Now that you have a list, how do you use it?

1. Use the qualities as a filter.

If something appears you think might be what you are looking for and does not have at least the first four qualities—with the first one first, it is not "it." Think of the time you will save if you can eliminate quickly and easily what is not right for you.

For example, if you find that safety is first on your quality list for a means of transportation and the car you are looking at has a very low safety record, don't buy this car no matter how much you love it. If you buy it, you will eventually be unhappy with it, and somehow you will unconsciously figure out how to get rid of it.

2. See the qualities everywhere.

See the qualities in everything, not just in what you're seeking. Notice that they're always with you in many forms. You have always had and always will have each quality on your list if you just look.

A quality does not have to belong to you. It can appear anywhere. All of what you see is already yours because you can see it. The goal is to notice that the quality you're looking for in an object already exists everywhere, and since you can see it—it exists for you—now.

3. Be grateful for each quality as you see it.

Be grateful for these qualities each time you see them, no matter where they occur.

If the person you dislike most has one of these qualities, be grateful that you have seen this quality in your life. Know that if it is "out there" it was first "within here" and therefore always available.

4. Be and live these qualities yourself.

Now that you have begun to live with God First, no longer is having the "thing" you wanted so important. You have discovered that it already exists as God's thoughts—qualities.

As we express gratitude, we are living in Grace. The result? Sometimes we realize we don't actually need the thing we were asking to see, or it turns up in another package, or it appears in a way greater than we could have dreamed.

Whichever way this happens, we have begun with seeking the kingdom of God first. That beginning cannot help but produce in our world whatever we need at the moment, because we began with the correct premise. We become conscious of always having whatever we need. We have never been abandoned, nor could we ever be. Looking for qualities opens your eyes to what has always been and always will be yours.

Forty-Four

Practical Blooming: Step Six

Thich Nhat Hanh said, *Our notions about happiness entrap us. We forget they are just ideas. Our idea of happiness can prevent us from actually being happy. We fail to see the opportunity for joy that is right in front of us when we are caught in a belief that happiness should take a particular form.*

And he offered this last piece of advice: *Do not lose yourself in the past. Do not lose yourself in the future. Do not get caught in your anger, worries, or fears. Come back to the present moment, and touch life deeply.*

1. What makes me discouraged?
2. Who or what is saying to me, "Naw Naw, it won't come up."
3. What can I let go of now?
4. What space in my life wants to be filled?
5. With what?
6. My heart is grateful for:
7. I am doing a quality word list on this:
PS:

Just a reminder that the place to find videos and more instructions on I Choose sheets and Quality Words are in the resource chapter of this book.

Forty-Five

Renee: Step Six

You are filtering reality. We need to open up and let go of the filters that are not serving us, filters of lack and scarcity, filters of not deserving healing, filters of not believing in miracles. These are the kinds of belief filters that we hold on to that prevent better things from happening in our life. — Anita Moorjani

For a few days, Renee was happier than she had ever been. Then she wasn't. Normally, she would have just ignored her feelings, but this time, she asked herself how she felt and listened to the answer.

She realized she felt depressed and discouraged. But first, she had been angry. Angry that nothing felt fun, that no one understood her, and she seemed to be alone even when she wasn't. When the anger faded, that's when she started feeling depressed and discouraged.

At first, it surprised Renee that she was angry. Perhaps if she had understood why she was angry, she wouldn't have slid into the other two emotions. At least if she was angry, she might do something about it.

But not when she was discouraged. That shut her down. It had never occurred to her that discouragement was the "devil's" tool. It seemed like a natural part of life. But what if it wasn't? For a moment, she got stuck in the question of if there was a devil, what it looked like, but realized that didn't help make her feel any better. In fact, she became more discouraged.

She decided to put those questions aside for when she felt more clear-headed and concentrate instead on getting undiscouraged. Besides, she wasn't sure anyone knew the answer to the question. She had heard once that the devil was only the claim, perception, and belief that God is not omnipotent. Renee thought that if that was true, it was essential to refute it by choosing a point of view that there was only one power, and it was Good.

It couldn't hurt, she told herself. She even remembered she needed to bring her state of mind into harmony with that point of view. To do that, she stood under a tree and felt its goodness and the community of nature that surrounded it.

Next, Renee did an I Choose sheet that said this: I desire to experience the omnipotence of Good.

Wow. That set off a firestorm of reasons that couldn't be true, at least not for her, which was laughable in a way. Did she think she was better than everyone else? That God didn't include her in his plan? As if she was important enough to be left out?

Laughing helped. It took away the power of discouragement, and she quickly came up with ideas to refute its claims. She kept the I Choose sheet running for a few days until the loud voice saying that she couldn't be happy, that she wasn't part of the Infinite Good, went silent—or at least she could barely hear it. Then she tore the sheet into little pieces and threw it away, feeling better than she had for as long as she could remember.

After that, answering the rest of the questions was easier. And Renee was grateful that she was growing and blooming in her own timing. Besides, what was the rush?

Renee chose to do a quality word list on how she would feel if she felt happy. The first word that popped into her head was *peaceful*. Other quality words came quickly after that, and she realized that sometimes she felt happy and hadn't noticed.

Realizing that she needed to put her quality word list in order and needed help to do it, she thought through all the people she knew who could do that for her. Finally, she settled on someone she knew at work who seemed open to such things.

She took the list of how to order quality words to work the next day and asked. It surprised her how happy the person was to be asked, and after the list was ordered, they spent time talking.

Renee added having a friendly conversation to her what-makes-me-happy list. And then, with an ordered quality word list in hand, she started using it.

To her surprise, the most challenging part of it all was letting go of how she thought things were and becoming open to the possibility that Good was omnipresent and omnipotent.

But it did not discourage her. She would get there because she was in charge of how she looked at things. That she could do.

Step Seven: Celebrate The Unique Bloom That You Are

Forty-Six

Stop Resisting

To believe in God for me is to feel that there is a God, not a dead one, or a stuffed one, but a living one, who with irresistible force urges us toward more loving. — Vincent Van Gogh

Nothing can stop a rose from being a rose, can it? If a rose could see outside itself and could abuse itself as we can, it may wish it was smaller, lived in the shade, and bloomed in the snow.

However, no amount of wishing will make that happen.

Relaxing and releasing into being a rose, it finds its unique spiritual blessing and joyfully allows itself to bloom. There is no work involved but to let go and be what it is, a rose.

Resisting what we are is so much work. Imagine an apple tree trying to be a grapevine or a violet wasting its life trying to be a lilac. No matter how much they try, they can't do it.

They could convince themselves that it was working, but all of us looking at the tree and violet would only see what they were—unless they did an outstanding job of putting up an illusion, so we could only see the lie.

But this is something humans are good at, producing and living within illusions. Plants—not so much.

In the world today, many people find it easier to succumb to the illusion of the worldview of "how things are." But that doesn't mean we have to play that perception game with them.

We have a choice. It is our perception that determines our reality. Not our self-will. Our perception. No matter how hard we try, we cannot change the Truth of omnipresent abundance to lack.

However, we can allow ourselves to be blinded by the propagated perception of lack. Then we struggle to survive and trade in our freedom of choice for the prison of limited perception.

Many will say "naw, naw," it won't come up. But they are wrong. It has, it is, and it will.

Don't listen to those that don't expect to grow. Inspire them instead by not taking part in the worldview game of fear, sorrow, and lack and move yourself out of those poor growing conditions.

You don't need to experience the bad to experience the good. This is another lie designed to keep us in the cycle of good to bad, from bad to good, sorrow to joy, and back to sorrow. That is not what happens in omnipresent Good.

We can learn from what appears as "bad" if it occurs, but there is no need to suffer to grow in wisdom and understanding.

Instead of the false perception of the need to experience bad to experience good, think of it this way.

There is the experience of good snuggling by the fire in the deepest of winter. And there is the experience of good swinging in a hammock under a shady tree in the summer. We don't have to make one wrong to enjoy the other.

Both experiences are qualities of the Infinite to enjoy and celebrate with gratitude, and in this way, we overcome the devil's tool of discouragement.

We absolutely don't need tragedy to experience omnipresent good. That is a perception that does not serve anyone.

Let your life have a bigger purpose than your ego. Find out who you are and be of service with it. Make yourself visible so others can benefit from what you offer. Accept payment and give payment abundantly.

Albert Einstein said, *Only a life lived for others is worth living.*

As you bloom into your life, this becomes self-evident and part of the joy of blooming as your unique spiritual blessing.

When you become aware that the Master Gardener is blooming Itself as you and that you are entirely necessary for the garden of life to be complete, all anxiety and fear will fade.

Shifting happens moment by moment, thought by thought. The results of this shift from a limited perception to an unlimited and omnipresent good perception far outweigh any time and effort we put into this practice.

Forty-Seven

Go For The Goodness

No one is useless in this world who lightens the burden of it for anyone else. — Charles Dickens

My daughter's family had a rescue dog named Eva. She was a kind, gentle, loving, and a very happy dog.

Watching her, one might have thought that Eva had an easy and happy puppy-hood, but that wasn't the case at all. In fact, it was completely the opposite. It was hard, mean, and by all appearances, cold and lonely.

However, instead of dwelling on her past, Eva went for the goodness. As she lived with her new family, she increased her goodness.

I understand that many rescue dogs are like Eva. They go for the goodness with all of their being.

However, we don't appear to be as good as Eva was at going for the goodness. Instead, we allow our past to direct our present, which is then the architect of our future.

Even though we have so many more opportunities and abilities to choose goodness than a dog does, we don't choose it. We dwell in past hurts, both true and perceived.

To add to the pain, we allow blame—not just to others—but also to ourselves, to fester and grow.

Remaining in this victim viewpoint in any degree leaves us in the same situation that we are trying to forget, or from which we wait to be rescued. However, unlike a dog that has to hope and wait for rescue, we can rescue our own lives and stop waiting for someone else to do it.

In fact, we must rescue our own lives, and not wait for another to do so, because no one else can. No one can "fix" us because it is our own hanging onto a past picture of lack of love that must be resolved if we want to be more like Eva—kind, gentle, loving, and happy.

The question is how to do this?

Most of us have a part of our past, whether it was yesterday's past or childhood pasts, which were painful. They weren't fair. They weren't kind, and they were not filled with joy.

How do we leave that memory, how do we forgive the players, how to we choose the now of happiness instead?

Viktor Frankl wrote: *A thought transfixed me: for the first time in my life I saw the truth as it is set into song by so many poets, proclaimed as the final wisdom by so many thinkers. The truth–that love is the ultimate and the highest goal to which man can aspire.*

With the goal of love in mind, how can we not go for the goodness?

As we rise to the awareness of Love's everywhere presence in the turn of a flower petal, the shape of a leaf, the smile of a child, the dew on the grass, the song of a bird, we begin to dissolve the need to hold on to and reciprocate with anger through either passive or aggressive choices.

What use is there in not forgiving? Can we see the stars when the earth is shrouded in fog? Neither can we see goodness within the fog of victim-hood.

We all yearn for world peace. However, how can there be world peace when there is not family peace? How can we wish for love to be known in everyone's heart when we don't know it within ours?

In order to forgive others and ourselves and reach for the awareness of Infinite Love, we have to rescue ourselves from the false claim of victim-hood. We have to aim for a higher love.

The sad story is that most victims become the abusers, sometimes physically, and always emotionally.

Perhaps it doesn't seem as if we are being abusive when we say we have a right to be sad, lonely, and depressed. However, for the people that love us, it is a hard thing to live with.

Sometimes we are abusive by punishing the other person who we feel has abused us, or other people that act like them, or remind us of them.

And, even if none of this is true for you, in victim-hood we are always abusive to ourselves.

We exist to share, live, and love Divine Love. Anything less than that, we are depriving ourselves of the infinite happiness that has been gifted to us as a result of our being.

We can rise higher. We can rise above the claims that exist within the worldview picture, and lift ourselves into the awareness and understanding that divine Love does not know abuse or lack.

Starting with this perfect sense of Love, we can make day-to-day choices that will begin to dissolve the pictures of abuse in all its forms, past, present, and future.

Let's all make Eva's choice and go for the goodness.

Let's all choose to make a higher love the architect of our future and rewrite the past, letting the hurt and anger dissolve into nothingness.

Forty-Eight

Be Unreasonably Happy

When a flower doesn't bloom you fix the environment in which it grows, not the flower.—Alexander den Heijer

We began walking this garden path understanding that we have a right to be happy, and a dawning awareness that we might have unconsciously chosen not to be.

We followed up with tools that help us recognize and let go of any conscious or unconscious ideas that keep us from living within and as happiness.

There is no reason to stop at a "sort of" happy place.

As we understand the true nature of Love as the only presence, the only activity, the only cause, and creator, then the mist of false perceptions of what claims to be situations and circumstances that produce unhappiness will dissolve.

This allows us to see happiness as a fundamental element and quality of life.

With this understanding of happiness, we eliminated all the reasons for unhappiness in one fell swoop, because they all begin and end from the false premise of duality and separation.

Now that you have prepared the soil, found the perfect place to bloom, watered and fed yourself with what suited you, and relaxed into your personal timing and growth, don't let those old beliefs and perceptions back in.

Be careful about what you choose to perceive.

Don't buy all that stuff and nonsense that claims that suffering is necessary and that we must be unhappy to be good or even to experience happiness. Realize that happiness is a quality of the Divine, as is Harmony. And Love.

When we experience less than happiness, it's not because it doesn't still exist. It's because we have misplaced our awareness of big R Reality. There is nothing to create. Nothing to get back to. Only the letting go of cherished, unconsciously or consciously, stubborn beliefs that hide happiness.

Happiness is experienced in a multitude of ways—an infinite variety of colors. But always we can choose it because in choosing it, we are stepping into the river of God's Joy.

If you were happy, how would you feel? Notice that those qualities are qualities of God. Which means we can't lose them. They are infinitely omnipresent.

Check your garden often for the weeds of discouragement and discontent to make sure unhappiness has not slipped back in without your noticing.

Daily, give yourself full permission to be utterly and unreasonably happy.

Pull out your list of what makes you happy once in a while and do something on it. Sing with the birds at least once a season, and experience what they know.

Continue with this happiness shift so that when you ask, "Who is the happiest person I know?" you will answer without hesitation, "It is me!"

And because you are the happiest person you know, it will be easy to include everyone into your circle of joy so everyone can answer the question the same way. "It's me." And that will be true.

Celebrate happiness every day and watch what happens.

In the spring, the plant called Spring Beauties pops up everywhere. It spreads like crazy. Most of the year, unless you know what to look for, you won't see it. But April and May in the east, you'll say, "What's that," and point to the lawn, and there they will be—spreading tremendous joy at the coming of spring. Tiny flowers with a big message.

Yes, you all are spring beauties: multiple colors and shapes, but all with a big message. Happiness is available to everyone at all times and does not need fanfare or admiration to be present.

You all are gifts of joy to the world. Go ahead, be happy about that!

You have prepared your garden for your future self. Now your "job" is to watch, water, weed, and enjoy the fruits of what you have done.

And as you know, there is always more growth, more perception shifting, and more to enjoy. That's the good news. We are not striving for completion. We are blooming into each day, being unreasonably happy.

Forty-Nine

Practical Blooming: Step Seven

In order to be irreplaceable one must always be different. — Coco Chanel

Remember, find out who you are and be of service with it. Make yourself visible so others can benefit from what you offer. Remember accept payment and give payment abundantly.

Answer these questions:

1. What do I have to share?

2. Am I willing to be visible as the unique spiritual blessing that I am. Yes - Not Sure - No

3. Am I willing to appreciate good by staying in good. Yes - Not Sure - No

4. I am willing to shift to fully blooming as myself.

>>Continue doing I Choose sheets.

>>Remember to use your Quality Word lists.

>>>>Go back through the *Blooming Your Life* book and do it again! Life is a progression, not a stop sign. Gardens evolve and become more and more beautiful. This will happen to your life too as you continue to practice shifting your perceptions.

Fifty

Go Forth And Bloom

There is no duty we so much underrate as the duty of being happy. By being happy we sow anonymous benefits upon the world. — Robert Louis Stevenson

Prepare yourself, you have blooming to do!

When you become aware that the Master Gardener is blooming Itself as you, and that you are entirely necessary for the garden of life to be complete, then anxiety and fear will fade.

Shifting happens moment by moment, thought by thought, and the results of this shift from a limited perception to an unlimited and omnipresent good perception far outweigh any time and effort you put into this practice.

Remember, we talked about two of the seven steps to shift lives: Be Willing and Become Aware.

If you would like all seven steps and learn more about them, they are in the book Seven Steps To Right Thinking.

And now we are ready to see in one place all the *Seven Simple Steps For Experiencing Consistent Happiness* or *How To Thrive In Your Life By Knowing Who You Are And Living It On Purpose*:

1. Prepare to grow.

2. Put yourself where you grow best.

3. Move yourself if necessary.

4. Feed yourself with the best "food" available.

5. Grow in your own timing.

6. Expect to bloom.

7. Celebrate the unique bloom that you are.

I hope you will go back and read this book over and over again. Keep reviewing the steps, because each time you do, you are approaching it from a new normal.

And before we step out into the world blooming as our unique spiritual blessing, let's see how Renee is doing.

FIFTY-ONE

RENEE: STEP SEVEN

I think I could turn and live with animals, they are so placid and self-contain'd, / I stand and look at them long and long. / They do not sweat and whine about their condition, / They do not lie awake in the dark and weep for their sins, / They do not make me sick discussing their duty to God, / Not one is dissatisfied, not one is demented with the mania of owning things, / Not one kneels to another, nor to his kind that lived thousands of years ago, / Not one is respectable or unhappy over the whole earth. — Walt Whitman

Renee finished reading this book and doing the worksheets and felt a surge of hope and joy. Now she knew she was in control of how she saw things. She was not at the mercy of other people's points of view.

She understood that when people said cruel and unkind things to each other, they had not chosen to understand the omnipotence of Good and the joy that flowed from that. And although she could feel sorry for them and perhaps in some way be helpful, she was not responsible for their point of view and behavior.

She was responsible for her own. And if she continued to choose a point of view and state of mind that brought joy and contentment to her, it would spread out like a stone thrown into a pond.

Renee understood that living in guilt and shame did not heal anybody or anything. But choosing to be happy did.

Yes, I am willing to be happy, Renee said to herself. I choose a perception of omnipresent Good. And when something doesn't appear to be good, I can do something about it.

Renee took herself through the seven steps each day.

She was prepared to grow. She would put herself where she grew best in every moment. She'd move herself when necessary. Sometimes that was as simple as stepping away from someone being angry and abusive. Other times, she would have to move away from it.

She would feed herself the food of goodness and kindness, and with the abundance that brought her, she'd share it with others. Sometimes that was only a smile, other times a listening ear, and sometimes it meant physically helping.

Each day, Renee reminded herself that she, like all the other blooms in the world, grows in her own timing. And like a beautiful garden, there was always something and someone to celebrate and admire as they expressed their unique spiritual blessing.

Today I expect to bloom with more happiness and then share it, was Renee's favorite thing to say to herself.

And each night, before falling asleep, she would thank you for the day and the gifts she had been given. She could already feel the effects of doing that. It seemed her gifts were growing, or at least she was experiencing them more often.

Yes, there were days when things didn't go well. Renee still wasn't sure about her job or where she lived, but Renee trusted that she would know what to do and do it when the time was right.

Along the way, she met a few new friends who wanted to walk the garden path with her. Together, they started through the book again and often discussed their progress.

What Renee appreciated the most was the proof she felt every day that she could choose how she perceived the world. She was experiencing the world differently, and that was a beautiful thing.

Fifty-Two

Author Note

This book was a long time in the making. In my life, I have gone through these seven steps repeatedly, each time making my life garden just a little more beautiful.

It was spring as I finished writing this book, so it was perfect timing. I could see how true it is that growth is the propulsion of the universe. And it also reminded me that gardens are never done. They require attention. And that's not a bad thing.

What I love most, though, is that gardeners are about community and sharing, and since we are all gardeners of our own lives, I love that we can share our growth steps together.

The business garden that I am growing is an evergreen garden online where anyone can take my courses at anytime. Plus a community circle where gardeners of perception can meet and get help and support from like-minded souls.

Like all gardens, it's a work in progress and will require attention. But this book reminded me what our life is about. Growing. Blooming. And sharing joy and happiness.

I thank you for walking this garden path with me, and I look forward to seeing you back here again. I will be watching for you.

— Beca

PS: If you, like me, love quotes and would like a list of all the quotes in this book—I have you covered. You can find where to download the list in the resource chapter of this book.

Resources

More Help To Shift
- *Perception Shifting Courses*, the *Perception Circle*—where you will find someone to help you with your Quality Word lists—and videos on how to do many of the things we discussed in the book can be found at PerceptionU.com

- You can download the workbook for this book for free here: perceptionu.com/the-library/workbooks/

- The list of quotes from this book is here: becalewis.com/books/shift-series/blooming-your-life/or in the workbook section at PerceptionU.com

- All my books are at BecaLewis.com

Books About Nature
- Mary Reynolds: *The Garden Awakening: Designs to*

Nurture Our Land and Ourselves and Reclaiming the Wild Soul: How Earth's Landscapes Restore Us to Wholeness

- Michal Polin: *The Botany of Desire: A Plant's-Eye View of the World*

- Robin Wall Kimmerer: *Braiding Sweetgrass: Indigenous Wisdom, Scientific Knowledge and the Teachings of Plants*

- Suzanne Simard: *Finding the Mother Tree: Discovering the Wisdom of the Forest*

- Plant Intelligence and the Imaginal Realm: Beyond the Doors of Perception into the Dreaming of Earth

- The Lost Language of Plants: *The Ecological Importance of Plant Medicine to Life on Earth*

Self-Discovery Tools

These are a few profiles I use in teaching and coaching. You might also find them valuable. Just remember, they are not boxes or excuses. They are not answers. They are mirrors. They are tools to help you thrive in the garden of your life.
- Enneagram: eclecticenergies.com/enneagram/test

Then sign up for this email and get the one that matches your results. See if you agree. If you had two answers, and you are not sure which one is true, get both emails. subscriptions.enneagraminstitute.com/subscribers/create
- Myers Briggs. Take the test at the back of the book: *Please Understand Me.* There are a few tests online that aren't

accurate and are easily manipulated. Besides, the book will help you understand yourself and others. That's always a good thing. I made a copy of this test. If you would like it, just let me know.

- Clifton Strengths:
  gallup.com/cliftonstrengths/en/home.aspx

- Gene Keys: genekeys.com/free-profile/

- Carol Tuttle's Energy Guide:
  my.liveyourtruth.com/freecourse/

- Gretchen Rubin's:
  Questioner-Rebel-Obliger-Upholder:
  gretchenrubin.com/2014/03/quiz-are-you-an-upholder-a-questioner-a-rebel-or-an-obliger/

You can also find this list at PerceptionU.com

Acknowledgments

I could never write a book without the help of my friends and my book community.

Thank you, Jet Tucker, Jamie Lewis, Barbara Budan, and Diana Cormier for taking the time to do the final reader proof. You are a loyal and much-loved reader team.

Thank you to every other member of my Book Community who helps me make so many decisions that help the book be the best book possible.

And as always, thank you to my beloved husband, Del, for being my daily sounding board, for putting up with all my questions, my constant need to want to make things better, and for being the love of my life, in more than just this one lifetime.

Other Places To Find Beca

- Facebook: facebook.com/becalewiscreative
- Instagram: instagram.com/becalewis
- LinkedIn: linkedin.com/in/becalewis
- Youtube: www.youtube.com/c/becalewis
- Buy Books Direct: https://becalewis.org/

Also By Beca

The Rivers of Time Series: Women's Lit, Friendship, Small Town, Mystery, Magical Realism, Small Town Fiction
The Returning, The Awakening, The Rising

Follow Me Here: Women's Lit, Friendship, Small Town, Mystery, Magical Realism, Small Town Fiction

The Ruby Sisters Series: Women's Lit, Friendship, Mystery, Small Town Fiction
A Last Gift, After All This Time, And Then She Remembered, As If It Was Real, Almost Innocent

Stories From Doveland: Women's Lit, Friendship, Small Town, Mystery, Magical Realism, Small Town Fiction
Karass, Pragma, Jatismar, Exousia, Stemma, Paragnosis, In-Between, Missing, Out Of Nowhere

The Return To Erda Series: Fantasy
Shatterskin, Deadsweep, Abbadon, The Experiment

The Chronicles of Thamon: Fantasy
Banished, Betrayed, Discovered, Wren's Story

The Shift Series: Spiritual Self-Help

Living in Grace: The Shift to Spiritual Perception
The Daily Shift: Daily Lessons From Love To Money
The 4 Essential Questions: Choosing Spiritually Healthy Habits
The 28 Day Shift To Wealth: A Daily Prosperity Plan
The Intent Course: Say Yes To What Moves You
Imagination Mastery: A Workbook For Shifting Your Reality
Right Thinking: A Thoughtful System for Healing
Perception Mastery: Seven Steps To Lasting Change
Blooming Your Life: How To Experience Consistent Happiness

Perception Parables: Very short stories

Love's Silent Sweet Secret: A Fable About Love
Golden Chains And Silver Cords: A Fable About Letting Go

Advice / Journals

A Woman's ABC's of Life: Lessons in Love, Life, and Career from Those Who Learned The Hard Way
The Daily Nudge(s): So When Did You First Notice

About Beca

Beca writes books she hopes will change people's perceptions of themselves and the world, and open possibilities to things and ideas that are waiting to be seen and experienced.

At sixteen, Beca founded her own dance studio. Later, she received a Master's Degree in Dance in Choreography from UCLA and founded the Harbinger Dance Theatre, a multimedia dance company, while continuing to run her dance school.

After graduating—to better support her three children—Beca switched to the sales field, where she worked as an employee and independent contractor in many industries, excelling in each while perfecting and teaching her Shift System and writing books.

She joined the financial industry in 1983 and became an Associate Vice President of Investments at a major stock brokerage firm. She was a licensed Certified Financial Planner for over twenty years.

This diversity, along with a variety of life challenges, helped fuel the desire to share what she's learned by writing and speaking, hoping it will make a difference in other people's lives.

Beca grew up in State College, PA, with the dream of becoming a dancer and then a writer. She carried that dream forward as she fulfilled a childhood wish by moving to Southern California in 1968. Beca told her family she would never move back to the cold.

After living there for thirty-one years, she met her husband, Delbert Lee Piper, Sr., at a retreat in Virginia, and everything changed. They decided to find a place they could call their own, which sent them off traveling around the United States. They lived and worked in a few different places before returning to live in the cold once again near Del's family in a small town in Northeast Ohio, not too far from State College.

When not working and teaching together, they love to visit and play with their combined family of eight children and five grandchildren, walk, read, study, do yoga or taiji, feed birds, and work in their garden.

www.ingramcontent.com/pod-product-compliance
Lightning Source LLC
Chambersburg PA
CBHW050234120526
44590CB00016B/2079